THRIVE
in
2025

FINANCIAL
EMPOWERMENT
PLANNER

Renee Bobb

2025 Calendar and Financial Empowerment Planner

- 2025 Calendar
- Monthly Financial Empowerment Affirmations
- 20 Ways to Increase Your Income
- Six Daily Empowering Questions to Boost Your Income
- Monthly Budget Forms
- Daily Spending Tracking Forms
- Daily Income Tracking Forms

Copyright © 2024 by Renee Bobb

Business Coach Renee Bobb
(615) 753-5647
reneebobbtraining@gmail.com
www.ReneeBobbTraining.com
www.stan.store/reneebobbtraining
www.GrantFundingAcademy

INSTRUCTIONS:

1. Review the entire calendar before you get started.

2. Read the positive affirmation daily for each month.

3. Write down your financial goals for each month.

4. Read your goals daily. Visualize yourself achieving your goals. You have to believe it to achieve it.

5. Budgeting Builds Wealth Forms.

   - At the beginning of the month fill out your Budgeting Builds Wealth form.
   - The goal is for you to be crystal clear about what it costs you to live each month.
   - Fill out the budget list on the first of the month and the actual list at the end of the month.
   - The next step is to compare the two of them to see how close you are to knowing how much you are spending each month.
   - This form gives you the opportunity to lower or even cut out some of the expenses on things you don't use, like gym memberships, apps, and publication subscriptions.
   - You will also be able to see if you are being overcharged or if some bills are increasing monthly.

6. Track Your Spending Monthly.

   - For each month you have daily spending tracking forms.
   - Every time you spend money you want to write it down.
   - At the end of the month review your spending forms and you will be amazed as to how much money you are wasting.
   - Don't get discouraged at the end of the first month when you realize how much money you're wasting.

- Now that you know better you can do better.
- Identify the money wasters and get rid of them once and for all.
- Find better uses of your money such as building up your emergency fund, savings account, investing in the stock market, and/or purchasing some real estate.

7. Track Your Income Monthly.

- Use the income tracking form to track your daily income.
- The goal is to be clear about how much money is coming in.
- For some people this will be a true wake-up call.
- The goal always is to create a system where you have daily deposits of money.
- If you need a few ideas, review the 20 Ways to Increase Your Income list. It will provide you with some great ideas on how you can create daily income.

8. Review the 20 Ways to Increase Your Income list. On this list you will see a variety of things that you can do in order to generate more income. I strongly recommend that you research each suggestion and select the one that best fits your interest.

20 WAYS TO INCREASE
YOUR INCOME

If you're like many people, you may have a desire to increase your income. The goal is to create daily deposits, weekly, monthly, and yearly income that will last you a lifetime.

Here is a list of some traditional and creative ways to increase your income. Be sure to conduct thorough research to identify the best strategy for you.

1. Full-time job.

2. Ask your boss for a raise.

3. Part-time job.

4. Freelance your talents and skills. Check out www.fiverr.com, www.taskrabbit.com, or www.Thumbtack.com.

5. Turn your passion into profits by starting your own business. Get a copy of "Start Smart: Your Guide to Starting and Growing a Business in 2025." www.ReneeBobbTraining.com

6. If you're a Military Veteran, file for your VA disability.

7. Share your areas of expertise by teaching classes at your local Adult Education Center or online. Check out my favorite platform Skool https://www.skool.com/refer?ref=9bd2f775915543909217859401014bb4A

    Here are a few other online platforms are: www.SkillShare.com, www.Udemy.com, or www.Teachable.com.

8. Launch a Crowdfunding Campaign on an online platforms such as: www.Kickstarters.com, www.GoFundMe.com, www.iFundWomen.com, or www.Indiegogo.com.

Crowdfunding is the practice of funding a project or venture by raising monetary contributions from a large number of people, typically via the internet.

9. If you have not used an item in your house in one year, then LET IT GO. Check out www.letitgo.com.

10. If you love dogs, why not become a dog walker? Check out www.Rover.com or www.Wag.com.

11. Collect back child support and/or alimony.

12. Register with at least three Temporary to Permanent agencies.

13. Rent out a room in your home (Airbnb).

14. Drive for Uber or Lyft.

15. Deliver food for Grubhub or Postmates.

16. Sell your photos on websites like Shutterstock, iStock, or Adobe.

17. It's time to tell your story. How about writing and publishing your own book? Check out www.ReneeBobbTraining.com for more information.

18. Rent out your car. Check out www.GetAround.com, www.RelayRides.com or www.Turo.com

19. Recycle your old cell phones.

20. Sell your handmade items and crafts on www.etsy.com or https://www.shopify.com/

JANUARY 2025

Financial Goal for January 2025: _____

_____

SUN	MON	TUE	WED	THU	FRI	SAT
			1	2	3	4
5	6	7	8	9	10	11
12	13	14	15	16	17	18
19	20	21	22	23	24	25
26	27	28	29	30	31	

SIX DAILY EMPOWERING QUESTIONS TO BOOST YOUR INCOME

Question 1: Discover Hidden Treasures: Each day, embark on a treasure hunt within your life. Ask yourself: What valuable possessions or assets can I offer for sale today? Share these gems on digital marketplaces and enlist the support of your warm network of friends and family to help you broadcast the news. Their assistance can be the catalyst for spreading the word far and wide.

_____

_____

_____

Question 2: Settle Past Accounts: Revisit your financial history and remind yourself of any outstanding debts owed to you. Reach out to these individuals and ensure that you collect what is rightfully yours.

_____

_____

_____

Question 3: Crafting Value to Share: Explore your artistic side and inquire: What valuable creations can I craft to share with others? Think about crafting handmade goods or offering digital prints as prime examples of how your creativity can translate into financial gains.

_____

_____

_____

_____

Question 4: Unleash Your Skills for Profit: Unleash your inner entrepreneur by pondering the following: What simple services can I provide in exchange for income? Consider your unique abilities, from mowing lawns and providing handyman services to diving into social media marketing, making calls, offering business coaching, consulting services, or administrative wizardry. Capitalize on your talents that have garnered admiration, as they can swiftly translate into a source of cash flow.

_____

_____

_____

Question 5: Solve Problems for Profit: Channel your creativity by asking: What common problems can I effortlessly solve? Identify your exceptional qualifications, talents, and skills that can be harnessed to generate swift income.

_____

_____

_____

Question 6: Trust in Networking: Lastly, consider your network of trustworthy connections. Is there someone you trust, and who trusts you, from whom you can secure a short-term loan if needed? Building on established relationships can provide vital financial support when you need it most.

_____

_____

_____

Your daily engagement with these questions can be a transformative step towards enhancing your financial well-being. Embrace the opportunity to unlock your financial potential!"

UNLOCKING FINANCIAL PROSPERITY THROUGH BUDGETING

Welcome to the path of financial empowerment. To take control of your financial destiny, harness the power of budgeting with the following guidance:

Step 1: Crafting Your Monthly Budget: Begin your journey by utilizing the form provided to create a comprehensive monthly budget. Initiate the process by documenting all your sources of income, leaving no potential revenue stream unaccounted for.

Step 2: Financial Planning: Start by being very clear about what you intend to spend during the course of the month. This includes allocating funds for essential categories such as housing, utilities, groceries, transportation, entertainment, and any other anticipated expenses.

Step 3: Analyzing Real-World Expenditure: At the end of the month, engage in an exercise of tracking your actual spending across various expense categories. This crucial step allows you to ascertain how closely your financial reality aligns with your initial budgetary projections.

Step 4: Prepare for Astonishing Revelations: As you compare your Total Monthly Income against both your Total Monthly Expenses and your Total Actual Spending, you may find yourself astounded. This insightful exercise often unveils a stark contrast between your perception of spending and the fiscal reality you have experienced.

Step 5: Harness the Power of Budgeting: Budgeting serves as a formidable instrument to commandeer your financial destiny. By consistently monitoring your income and expenses, you empower yourself to make informed financial decisions. As a result, you pave the way for building wealth and achieving the financial prosperity you aspire to attain."

MONTHLY INCOME AND EXPENSES WORKSHEET

Monthly Income Per Month

Products   _____ $_____

Services   _____ $_____

Other Income

Bonus $_____

Commission $_____

Grants $_____

Other $_____ $_____

Other $_____ $_____

Total Income $_____

BUDGETING BUILDS WEALTH

Use the form below to create your monthly budget. Start by writing down what you plan to spend for the month. At the end of the month, write in what you actually spent for the month and then compare the two lists. You will be amazed at how much you think you are spending compared to what you are actually have spent.

Monthly Expenses	Budget	Actual
Salary	_____	_____
Mortgage or Rent	_____	_____
Insurance	_____	_____
Appliance Payments	_____	_____
Cable	_____	_____
Taxes	_____	_____
Electricity	_____	_____
Gas	_____	_____
Water	_____	_____
Trash/Recycle/Sewage	_____	_____
Telephone (Office)	_____	_____
Cell Phone	_____	_____
Internet	_____	_____
Office Maintenance	_____	_____
Food (Eating Out)	_____	_____
Automobile Payment	_____	_____

Gas and Oil   _____   _____

Car Insurance   _____   _____

License   _____   _____

Automobile Repairs   _____   _____

Life Insurance   _____   _____

Medical Insurance   _____   _____

Childcare   _____   _____

Savings/Investments   _____   _____

Clothing   _____   _____

Dry Cleaning/Laundry   _____   _____

Printing   _____   _____

Office/Cleaning Supplies   _____   _____

Tuition/Education   _____   _____

Dues/Memberships   _____   _____

Gifts   _____   _____

Apps/Subscriptions   _____   _____

Books and Magazines   _____   _____

Entertainment   _____   _____

Travel   _____   _____

Marketing and Advertising   _____   _____

Total Expenses $_____ $_____

FINANCIAL REALITY TOTAL

Monthly Income $_____

       Subtract

Total Expenses $_____

     Surplus + $_____

     Deficit - $_____

Do you have a surplus or a deficit at the end of the month?

_____Surplus   _____Deficit

If you are spending more than you earn, there are some major changes that need to take place.

How can you increase your income?

1.   6.

2.   7.

3.   8.

4.   9.

5.   10.

How can you cut your spending? What are the items that you can do without?

1.   6.

2.   7.

3.   8.

4.   9.

5.   10.

TRACK YOUR SPENDING

It's very important that you track your spending on this journey. You must be aware of where each and every penny is going. Use the forms below to track your daily spending. The goal is to get rid of wasteful spending and plan for your financial future.

DAILY SPENDING RECORD
JANUARY 2025

Week Start Date: _____ **Week End Date:** _____

Date: Amount:	Date: Amount:
Item:	Item:
Date: Amount:	Date: Amount:
Item:	Item:
Date: Amount:	Date: Amount:
Item:	Item:
Date: Amount:	Date: Amount:
Item:	Item:
Date: Amount:	Date: Amount:
Item:	Item:
Date: Amount:	Date: Amount:
Item:	Item:
Number of Items for the Day:	**Total Amount Spent:**

DAILY SPENDING RECORD
JANUARY 2025

Week Start Date: _____ **Week End Date:** _____

Date: Amount:	Date: Amount:
Item:	Item:
Date: Amount:	Date: Amount:
Item:	Item:
Date: Amount:	Date: Amount:
Item:	Item:
Date: Amount:	Date: Amount:
Item:	Item:
Date: Amount:	Date: Amount:
Item:	Item:
Date: Amount:	Date: Amount:
Item:	Item:
Number of Items for the Day:	**Total Amount Spent:**

DAILY SPENDING RECORD
JANUARY 2025

Week Start Date: _____ **Week End Date:** _____

Date: Amount:	Date: Amount:
Item:	Item:
Date: Amount:	Date: Amount:
Item:	Item:
Date: Amount:	Date: Amount:
Item:	Item:
Date: Amount:	Date: Amount:
Item:	Item:
Date: Amount:	Date: Amount:
Item:	Item:
Date: Amount:	Date: Amount:
Item:	Item:
Number of Items for the Day:	**Total Amount Spent:**

DAILY SPENDING RECORD
JANUARY 2025

Week Start Date: _____ **Week End Date:** _____

Date:	Amount:	Date:	Amount:
Item:		Item:	
Date:	Amount:	Date:	Amount:
Item:		Item:	
Date:	Amount:	Date:	Amount:
Item:		Item:	
Date:	Amount:	Date:	Amount:
Item:		Item:	
Date:	Amount:	Date:	Amount:
Item:		Item:	
Date:	Amount:	Date:	Amount:
Item:		Item:	
Number of Items for the Day:		**Total Amount Spent:**	

DAILY SPENDING RECORD
JANUARY 2025

Week Start Date: _____ **Week End Date:** _____

Date:	Amount:	Date:	Amount:
Item:		Item:	
Date:	Amount:	Date:	Amount:
Item:		Item:	
Date:	Amount:	Date:	Amount:
Item:		Item:	
Date:	Amount:	Date:	Amount:
Item:		Item:	
Date:	Amount:	Date:	Amount:
Item:		Item:	
Date:	Amount:	Date:	Amount:
Item:		Item:	
Number of Items for the Day:		**Total Amount Spent:**	

Set a goal to make 2025 the year of abundance. Use the form below to track every penny that you're receiving. It's amazing that when your mind is focused on abundance, you begin to create abundance.

DAILY INCOME RECORD
JANUARY 2025

	Date	Source	Amount
1			
2			
3			
4			
5			
6			
7			
8			
9			
10			
11			
12			
13			
14			
15			
16			
17			
18			
19			
20			
21			
22			
23			
24			
25			
26			
27			
28			
29			
30			
31			

CULTIVATE AN ATTITUDE OF GRATITUDE

Everyday take 10 to 15 minutes to write down a few things you are grateful for. Don't just write things down really feel what you are writing. The more grateful you are the more financial blessings will come your way. I am speaking from my own experience. Try it, it really works.

1. _____

2. _____

3. _____

4. _____

5. _____

6. _____

7. _____

8. _____

9. _____

10. _____

11. _____

12. _____

13. _____

14. _____

15. _____

16. _____

17. _____

18. _____

19. _____

20 _____

FEBRUARY 2025

Financial Goal for February 2025: _____

_____

SUN	MON	TUE	WED	THU	FRI	SAT
						1
2	3	4	5	6	7	8
9	10	11	12	13	14	15
16	17	18	19	20	21	22
23	24	25	26	27	28	

SIX DAILY EMPOWERING QUESTIONS TO BOOST YOUR INCOME

Question 1: Discover Hidden Treasures: Each day, embark on a treasure hunt within your life. Ask yourself: What valuable possessions or assets can I offer for sale today? Share these gems on digital marketplaces and enlist the support of your warm network of friends and family to help you broadcast the news. Their assistance can be the catalyst for spreading the word far and wide.

_____

_____

_____

Question 2: Settle Past Accounts: Revisit your financial history and remind yourself of any outstanding debts owed to you. Reach out to these individuals and ensure that you collect what is rightfully yours.

_____

_____

_____

Question 3: Crafting Value to Share: Explore your artistic side and inquire: What valuable creations can I craft to share with others? Think about crafting handmade goods or offering digital prints as prime examples of how your creativity can translate into financial gains.

_____

_____

_____

_____

Question 4: Unleash Your Skills for Profit: Unleash your inner entrepreneur by pondering the following: What simple services can I provide in exchange for income? Consider your unique abilities, from mowing lawns and providing handyman services to diving into social media marketing, making calls, offering business coaching, consulting services, or administrative wizardry. Capitalize on your talents that have garnered admiration, as they can swiftly translate into a source of cash flow.

_____

_____

_____

Question 5: Solve Problems for Profit: Channel your creativity by asking: What common problems can I effortlessly solve? Identify your exceptional qualifications, talents, and skills that can be harnessed to generate swift income.

_____

_____

_____

Question 6: Trust in Networking: Lastly, consider your network of trustworthy connections. Is there someone you trust, and who trusts you, from whom you can secure a short-term loan if needed? Building on established relationships can provide vital financial support when you need it most.

_____

_____

_____

Your daily engagement with these questions can be a transformative step towards enhancing your financial well-being. Embrace the opportunity to unlock your financial potential!"

UNLOCKING FINANCIAL PROSPERITY THROUGH BUDGETING

Welcome to the path of financial empowerment. To take control of your financial destiny, harness the power of budgeting with the following guidance:

Step 1: Crafting Your Monthly Budget: Begin your journey by utilizing the form provided to create a comprehensive monthly budget. Initiate the process by documenting all your sources of income, leaving no potential revenue stream unaccounted for.

Step 2: Financial Planning: Start by being very clear about what you intend to spend during the course of the month. This includes allocating funds for essential categories such as housing, utilities, groceries, transportation, entertainment, and any other anticipated expenses.

Step 3: Analyzing Real-World Expenditure: At the end of the month, engage in an exercise of tracking your actual spending across various expense categories. This crucial step allows you to ascertain how closely your financial reality aligns with your initial budgetary projections.

Step 4: Prepare for Astonishing Revelations: As you compare your Total Monthly Income against both your Total Monthly Expenses and your Total Actual Spending, you may find yourself astounded. This insightful exercise often unveils a stark contrast between your perception of spending and the fiscal reality you have experienced.

Step 5: Harness the Power of Budgeting: Budgeting serves as a formidable instrument to commandeer your financial destiny. By consistently monitoring your income and expenses, you empower yourself to make informed financial decisions. As a result, you pave the way for building wealth and achieving the financial prosperity you aspire to attain."

MONTHLY INCOME AND EXPENSES WORKSHEET

Monthly Income Per Month

Products _____ $_____

Services _____ $_____

Other Income

Bonus $_____

Commission $_____

Grants $_____

Other $_____ $_____

Other $_____ $_____

Total Income $_____

BUDGETING BUILDS WEALTH

Use the form below to create your monthly budget. Start by writing down what you plan to spend for the month. At the end of the month, write in what you actually spent for the month and then compare the two lists. You will be amazed at how much you think you are spending compared to what you are actually have spent.

Monthly Expenses	Budget	Actual
Salary	_____	_____
Mortgage or Rent	_____	_____
Insurance	_____	_____
Appliance Payments	_____	_____
Cable	_____	_____
Taxes	_____	_____
Electricity	_____	_____
Gas	_____	_____
Water	_____	_____
Trash/Recycle/Sewage	_____	_____
Telephone (Office)	_____	_____
Cell Phone	_____	_____
Internet	_____	_____
Office Maintenance	_____	_____
Food (Eating Out)	_____	_____
Automobile Payment	_____	_____

Gas and Oil	_____	_____
Car Insurance	_____	_____
License	_____	_____
Automobile Repairs	_____	_____
Life Insurance	_____	_____
Medical Insurance	_____	_____
Childcare	_____	_____
Savings/Investments	_____	_____
Clothing	_____	_____
Dry Cleaning/Laundry	_____	_____
Printing	_____	_____
Office/Cleaning Supplies	_____	_____
Tuition/Education	_____	_____
Dues/Memberships	_____	_____
Gifts	_____	_____
Apps/Subscriptions	_____	_____
Books and Magazines	_____	_____
Entertainment	_____	_____
Travel	_____	_____
Marketing and Advertising	_____	_____
Total Expenses	$_____	$_____

FINANCIAL REALITY TOTAL

Monthly Income $_____

     Subtract

Total Expenses $_____

     Surplus + $_____

     Deficit - $_____

Do you have a surplus or a deficit at the end of the month?

_____Surplus   _____Deficit

If you are spending more than you earn, there are some major changes that need to take place.

How can you increase your income?

1.   6.

2.   7.

3.   8.

4.   9.

5.   10.

How can you cut your spending? What are the items that you can do without?

1.   6.

2.   7.

3.   8.

4.   9.

5.   10.

TRACK YOUR SPENDING

It's very important that you track your spending on this journey. You must be aware of where each and every penny is going. Use the forms below to track your daily spending. The goal is to get rid of wasteful spending and plan for your financial future.

DAILY SPENDING RECORD
FEBRUARY 2025

Week Start Date: _____ **Week End Date:** _____

Date: Amount: Item:	Date: Amount: Item:	
Date: Amount: Item:	Date: Amount: Item:	
Date: Amount: Item:	Date: Amount: Item:	
Date: Amount: Item:	Date: Amount: Item:	
Date: Amount: Item:	Date: Amount: Item:	
Date: Amount: Item:	Date: Amount: Item:	
Number of Items for the Day:	**Total Amount Spent:**	

DAILY SPENDING RECORD
FEBRUARY 2025

Week Start Date: _____ **Week End Date:** _____

Date: Amount:	Date: Amount:
Item:	Item:
Date: Amount:	Date: Amount:
Item:	Item:
Date: Amount:	Date: Amount:
Item:	Item:
Date: Amount:	Date: Amount:
Item:	Item:
Date: Amount:	Date: Amount:
Item:	Item:
Date: Amount:	Date: Amount:
Item:	Item:
Number of Items for the Day:	**Total Amount Spent:**

DAILY SPENDING RECORD
FEBRUARY 2025

Week Start Date: _____ **Week End Date:** _____

Date: Amount:	Date: Amount:
Item:	Item:
Date: Amount:	Date: Amount:
Item:	Item:
Date: Amount:	Date: Amount:
Item:	Item:
Date: Amount:	Date: Amount:
Item:	Item:
Date: Amount:	Date: Amount:
Item:	Item:
Date: Amount:	Date: Amount:
Item:	Item:
Number of Items for the Day:	**Total Amount Spent:**

DAILY SPENDING RECORD
FEBRUARY 2025

Week Start Date: _____   **Week End Date:** _____

Date:	Amount:	Date:	Amount:
Item:		Item:	
Date:	Amount:	Date:	Amount:
Item:		Item:	
Date:	Amount:	Date:	Amount:
Item:		Item:	
Date:	Amount:	Date:	Amount:
Item:		Item:	
Date:	Amount:	Date:	Amount:
Item:		Item:	
Date:	Amount:	Date:	Amount:
Item:		Item:	
Number of Items for the Day:		**Total Amount Spent:**	

DAILY SPENDING RECORD
FEBRUARY 2025

Week Start Date: _____   **Week End Date:** _____

Date:	Amount:	Date:	Amount:
Item:		Item:	
Date:	Amount:	Date:	Amount:
Item:		Item:	
Date:	Amount:	Date:	Amount:
Item:		Item:	
Date:	Amount:	Date:	Amount:
Item:		Item:	
Date:	Amount:	Date:	Amount:
Item:		Item:	
Date:	Amount:	Date:	Amount:
Item:		Item:	
Number of Items for the Day:		**Total Amount Spent:**	

Set a goal to make 2025 the year of abundance. Use the form below to track every penny that you're receiving. It's amazing that when your mind is focused on abundance, you begin to create abundance.

DAILY INCOME RECORD
FEBRUARY 2025

	Date	Source	Amount
1			
2			
3			
4			
5			
6			
7			
8			
9			
10			
11			
12			
13			
14			
15			
16			
17			
18			
19			
20			
21			
22			
23			
24			
25			
26			
27			
28			

CULTIVATE AN ATTITUDE OF GRATITUDE

Everyday take 10 to 15 minutes to write down a few things you are grateful for. Don't just write things down really feel what you are writing. The more grateful you are the more financial blessings will come your way. I am speaking from my own experience. Try it, it really works.

1. _____
2. _____
3. _____
4. _____
5. _____
6. _____
7. _____
8. _____
9. _____
10. _____
11. _____
12. _____
13. _____
14. _____
15. _____
16. _____
17. _____
18. _____
19. _____
20 _____

MARCH 2025

Financial Goal for March 2025: _____

_____

SUN	MON	TUE	WED	THU	FRI	SAT
						1
2	3	4	5	6	7	8
9	10	11	12	13	14	15
16	17	18	19	20	21	22
23	24	25	26	27	28	29
30	31					

SIX DAILY EMPOWERING QUESTIONS TO BOOST YOUR INCOME

Question 1: Discover Hidden Treasures: Each day, embark on a treasure hunt within your life. Ask yourself: What valuable possessions or assets can I offer for sale today? Share these gems on digital marketplaces and enlist the support of your warm network of friends and family to help you broadcast the news. Their assistance can be the catalyst for spreading the word far and wide.

_____

_____

_____

Question 2: Settle Past Accounts: Revisit your financial history and remind yourself of any outstanding debts owed to you. Reach out to these individuals and ensure that you collect what is rightfully yours.

_____

_____

_____

Question 3: Crafting Value to Share: Explore your artistic side and inquire: What valuable creations can I craft to share with others? Think about crafting handmade goods or offering digital prints as prime examples of how your creativity can translate into financial gains.

_____

_____

_____

_____

Question 4: Unleash Your Skills for Profit: Unleash your inner entrepreneur by pondering the following: What simple services can I provide in exchange for income? Consider your unique abilities, from mowing lawns and providing handyman services to diving into social media marketing, making calls, offering business coaching, consulting services, or administrative wizardry. Capitalize on your talents that have garnered admiration, as they can swiftly translate into a source of cash flow.

_____

_____

_____

Question 5: Solve Problems for Profit: Channel your creativity by asking: What common problems can I effortlessly solve? Identify your exceptional qualifications, talents, and skills that can be harnessed to generate swift income.

_____

_____

_____

Question 6: Trust in Networking: Lastly, consider your network of trustworthy connections. Is there someone you trust, and who trusts you, from whom you can secure a short-term loan if needed? Building on established relationships can provide vital financial support when you need it most.

_____

_____

_____

Your daily engagement with these questions can be a transformative step towards enhancing your financial well-being. Embrace the opportunity to unlock your financial potential!"

UNLOCKING FINANCIAL PROSPERITY THROUGH BUDGETING

Welcome to the path of financial empowerment. To take control of your financial destiny, harness the power of budgeting with the following guidance:

Step 1: Crafting Your Monthly Budget: Begin your journey by utilizing the form provided to create a comprehensive monthly budget. Initiate the process by documenting all your sources of income, leaving no potential revenue stream unaccounted for.

Step 2: Financial Planning: Start by being very clear about what you intend to spend during the course of the month. This includes allocating funds for essential categories such as housing, utilities, groceries, transportation, entertainment, and any other anticipated expenses.

Step 3: Analyzing Real-World Expenditure: At the end of the month, engage in an exercise of tracking your actual spending across various expense categories. This crucial step allows you to ascertain how closely your financial reality aligns with your initial budgetary projections.

Step 4: Prepare for Astonishing Revelations: As you compare your Total Monthly Income against both your Total Monthly Expenses and your Total Actual Spending, you may find yourself astounded. This insightful exercise often unveils a stark contrast between your perception of spending and the fiscal reality you have experienced.

Step 5: Harness the Power of Budgeting: Budgeting serves as a formidable instrument to commandeer your financial destiny. By consistently monitoring your income and expenses, you empower yourself to make informed financial decisions. As a result, you pave the way for building wealth and achieving the financial prosperity you aspire to attain."

MONTHLY INCOME AND EXPENSES WORKSHEET

Monthly Income Per Month

Products   _____ $_____

Services   _____ $_____

Other Income

Bonus $_____

Commission $_____

Grants $_____

Other $_____ $_____

Other $_____ $_____

Total Income $_____

BUDGETING BUILDS WEALTH

Use the form below to create your monthly budget. Start by writing down what you plan to spend for the month. At the end of the month, write in what you actually spent for the month and then compare the two lists. You will be amazed at how much you think you are spending compared to what you are actually have spent.

Monthly Expenses	Budget	Actual
Salary	_____	_____
Mortgage or Rent	_____	_____
Insurance	_____	_____
Appliance Payments	_____	_____
Cable	_____	_____
Taxes	_____	_____
Electricity	_____	_____
Gas	_____	_____
Water	_____	_____
Trash/Recycle/Sewage	_____	_____
Telephone (Office)	_____	_____
Cell Phone	_____	_____
Internet	_____	_____
Office Maintenance	_____	_____
Food (Eating Out)	_____	_____
Automobile Payment	_____	_____

Gas and Oil	_____	_____
Car Insurance	_____	_____
License	_____	_____
Automobile Repairs	_____	_____
Life Insurance	_____	_____
Medical Insurance	_____	_____
Childcare	_____	_____
Savings/Investments	_____	_____
Clothing	_____	_____
Dry Cleaning/Laundry	_____	_____
Printing	_____	_____
Office/Cleaning Supplies	_____	_____
Tuition/Education	_____	_____
Dues/Memberships	_____	_____
Gifts	_____	_____
Apps/Subscriptions	_____	_____
Books and Magazines	_____	_____
Entertainment	_____	_____
Travel	_____	_____
Marketing and Advertising	_____	_____
Total Expenses	$_____	$_____

FINANCIAL REALITY TOTAL

Monthly Income $_____

      Subtract
Total Expenses $_____
    Surplus + $_____
    Deficit - $_____

Do you have a surplus or a deficit at the end of the month?
_____Surplus   _____Deficit

If you are spending more than you earn, there are some major changes that need to take place.

How can you increase your income?

1.   6.

2.   7.

3.   8.

4.   9.

5.   10.

How can you cut your spending? What are the items that you can do without?

1.   6.

2.   7.

3.   8.

4.   9.

5.   10.

TRACK YOUR SPENDING

It's very important that you track your spending on this journey. You must be aware of where each and every penny is going. Use the forms below to track your daily spending. The goal is to get rid of wasteful spending and plan for your financial future.

DAILY SPENDING RECORD
MARCH 2025

Week Start Date: _____ **Week End Date:** _____

Date: Amount: Item:	Date: Amount: Item:
Date: Amount: Item:	Date: Amount: Item:
Date: Amount: Item:	Date: Amount: Item:
Date: Amount: Item:	Date: Amount: Item:
Date: Amount: Item:	Date: Amount: Item:
Date: Amount: Item:	Date: Amount: Item:
Number of Items for the Day:	**Total Amount Spent:**

DAILY SPENDING RECORD
MARCH 2025

Week Start Date: _____ **Week End Date:** _____

Date: Amount:	Date: Amount:
Item:	Item:
Date: Amount:	Date: Amount:
Item:	Item:
Date: Amount:	Date: Amount:
Item:	Item:
Date: Amount:	Date: Amount:
Item:	Item:
Date: Amount:	Date: Amount:
Item:	Item:
Date: Amount:	Date: Amount:
Item:	Item:
Number of Items for the Day:	**Total Amount Spent:**

DAILY SPENDING RECORD
MARCH 2025

Week Start Date: _____ **Week End Date:** _____

Date: Amount:	Date: Amount:
Item:	Item:
Date: Amount:	Date: Amount:
Item:	Item:
Date: Amount:	Date: Amount:
Item:	Item:
Date: Amount:	Date: Amount:
Item:	Item:
Date: Amount:	Date: Amount:
Item:	Item:
Date: Amount:	Date: Amount:
Item:	Item:
Number of Items for the Day:	**Total Amount Spent:**

DAILY SPENDING RECORD
MARCH 2025

Week Start Date: _____ **Week End Date:** _____

Date: Item:	Amount:	Date: Item:	Amount:
Date: Item:	Amount:	Date: Item:	Amount:
Date: Item:	Amount:	Date: Item:	Amount:
Date: Item:	Amount:	Date: Item:	Amount:
Date: Item:	Amount:	Date: Item:	Amount:
Date: Item:	Amount:	Date: Item:	Amount:
Number of Items for the Day:		**Total Amount Spent:**	

DAILY SPENDING RECORD
MARCH 2025

Week Start Date: _____ **Week End Date:** _____

Date: Item:	Amount:	Date: Item:	Amount:
Date: Item:	Amount:	Date: Item:	Amount:
Date: Item:	Amount:	Date: Item:	Amount:
Date: Item:	Amount:	Date: Item:	Amount:
Date: Item:	Amount:	Date: Item:	Amount:
Date: Item:	Amount:	Date: Item:	Amount:
Number of Items for the Day:		**Total Amount Spent:**	

Set a goal to make 2025 the year of abundance. Use the form below to track every penny that you're receiving. It's amazing that when your mind is focused on abundance, you begin to create abundance.

DAILY INCOME RECORD
MARCH 2025

	Date	Source	Amount
1			
2			
3			
4			
5			
6			
7			
8			
9			
10			
11			
12			
13			
14			
15			
16			
17			
18			
19			
20			
21			
22			
23			
24			
25			
26			
27			
28			
29			
30			
31			

CULTIVATE AN ATTITUDE OF GRATITUDE

Everyday take 10 to 15 minutes to write down a few things you are grateful for. Don't just write things down really feel what you are writing. The more grateful you are the more financial blessings will come your way. I am speaking from my own experience. Try it, it really works.

1. _____
2. _____
3. _____
4. _____
5. _____
6. _____
7. _____
8. _____
9. _____
10. _____
11. _____
12. _____
13. _____
14. _____
15. _____
16. _____
17. _____
18. _____
19. _____
20 _____

APRIL 2025

Financial Goal for April 2025: _____

_____

SUN	MON	TUE	WED	THU	FRI	SAT
		1	2	3	4	5
6	7	8	9	10	11	12
13	14	15	16	17	18	19
20	21	22	23	24	25	26
27	28	29	30			

SIX DAILY EMPOWERING QUESTIONS TO BOOST YOUR INCOME

Question 1: Discover Hidden Treasures: Each day, embark on a treasure hunt within your life. Ask yourself: What valuable possessions or assets can I offer for sale today? Share these gems on digital marketplaces and enlist the support of your warm network of friends and family to help you broadcast the news. Their assistance can be the catalyst for spreading the word far and wide.

_____

_____

_____

Question 2: Settle Past Accounts: Revisit your financial history and remind yourself of any outstanding debts owed to you. Reach out to these individuals and ensure that you collect what is rightfully yours.

_____

_____

_____

Question 3: Crafting Value to Share: Explore your artistic side and inquire: What valuable creations can I craft to share with others? Think about crafting handmade goods or offering digital prints as prime examples of how your creativity can translate into financial gains.

_____

_____

_____

_____

Question 4: Unleash Your Skills for Profit: Unleash your inner entrepreneur by pondering the following: What simple services can I provide in exchange for income? Consider your unique abilities, from mowing lawns and providing handyman services to diving into social media marketing, making calls, offering business coaching, consulting services, or administrative wizardry. Capitalize on your talents that have garnered admiration, as they can swiftly translate into a source of cash flow.

_____

_____

_____

Question 5: Solve Problems for Profit: Channel your creativity by asking: What common problems can I effortlessly solve? Identify your exceptional qualifications, talents, and skills that can be harnessed to generate swift income.

_____

_____

_____

Question 6: Trust in Networking: Lastly, consider your network of trustworthy connections. Is there someone you trust, and who trusts you, from whom you can secure a short-term loan if needed? Building on established relationships can provide vital financial support when you need it most.

_____

_____

_____

Your daily engagement with these questions can be a transformative step towards enhancing your financial well-being. Embrace the opportunity to unlock your financial potential!"

UNLOCKING FINANCIAL PROSPERITY THROUGH BUDGETING

Welcome to the path of financial empowerment. To take control of your financial destiny, harness the power of budgeting with the following guidance:

Step 1: Crafting Your Monthly Budget: Begin your journey by utilizing the form provided to create a comprehensive monthly budget. Initiate the process by documenting all your sources of income, leaving no potential revenue stream unaccounted for.

Step 2: Financial Planning: Start by being very clear about what you intend to spend during the course of the month. This includes allocating funds for essential categories such as housing, utilities, groceries, transportation, entertainment, and any other anticipated expenses.

Step 3: Analyzing Real-World Expenditure: At the end of the month, engage in an exercise of tracking your actual spending across various expense categories. This crucial step allows you to ascertain how closely your financial reality aligns with your initial budgetary projections.

Step 4: Prepare for Astonishing Revelations: As you compare your Total Monthly Income against both your Total Monthly Expenses and your Total Actual Spending, you may find yourself astounded. This insightful exercise often unveils a stark contrast between your perception of spending and the fiscal reality you have experienced.

Step 5: Harness the Power of Budgeting: Budgeting serves as a formidable instrument to commandeer your financial destiny. By consistently monitoring your income and expenses, you empower yourself to make informed financial decisions. As a result, you pave the way for building wealth and achieving the financial prosperity you aspire to attain."

MONTHLY INCOME AND EXPENSES WORKSHEET

Monthly Income Per Month

Products   _____ $_____

Services   _____ $_____

Other Income

Bonus $_____

Commission $_____

Grants $_____

Other $_____ $_____

Other $_____ $_____

Total Income $_____

BUDGETING BUILDS WEALTH

Use the form below to create your monthly budget. Start by writing down what you plan to spend for the month. At the end of the month, write in what you actually spent for the month and then compare the two lists. You will be amazed at how much you think you are spending compared to what you are actually have spent.

Monthly Expenses	Budget	Actual
Salary	_____	_____
Mortgage or Rent	_____	_____
Insurance	_____	_____
Appliance Payments	_____	_____
Cable	_____	_____
Taxes	_____	_____
Electricity	_____	_____
Gas	_____	_____
Water	_____	_____
Trash/Recycle/Sewage	_____	_____
Telephone (Office)	_____	_____
Cell Phone	_____	_____
Internet	_____	_____
Office Maintenance	_____	_____
Food (Eating Out)	_____	_____
Automobile Payment	_____	_____

Gas and Oil	_____	_____
Car Insurance	_____	_____
License	_____	_____
Automobile Repairs	_____	_____
Life Insurance	_____	_____
Medical Insurance	_____	_____
Childcare	_____	_____
Savings/Investments	_____	_____
Clothing	_____	_____
Dry Cleaning/Laundry	_____	_____
Printing	_____	_____
Office/Cleaning Supplies	_____	_____
Tuition/Education	_____	_____
Dues/Memberships	_____	_____
Gifts	_____	_____
Apps/Subscriptions	_____	_____
Books and Magazines	_____	_____
Entertainment	_____	_____
Travel	_____	_____
Marketing and Advertising	_____	_____
Total Expenses	$_____	$_____

FINANCIAL REALITY TOTAL

Monthly Income $\$$_____

          Subtract

Total Expenses $\$$_____

      Surplus + $\$$_____

      Deficit - $\$$_____

Do you have a surplus or a deficit at the end of the month?

_____Surplus   _____Deficit

If you are spending more than you earn, there are some major changes that need to take place.

How can you increase your income?

1.   6.

2.   7.

3.   8.

4.   9.

5.   10.

How can you cut your spending? What are the items that you can do without?

1.   6.

2.   7.

3.   8.

4.   9.

5.   10.

TRACK YOUR SPENDING

It's very important that you track your spending on this journey. You must be aware of where each and every penny is going. Use the forms below to track your daily spending. The goal is to get rid of wasteful spending and plan for your financial future.

DAILY SPENDING RECORD
APRIL 2025

Week Start Date: _____ **Week End Date:** _____

Date: Amount:		Date: Amount:	
Item:		Item:	
Date: Amount:		Date: Amount:	
Item:		Item:	
Date: Amount:		Date: Amount:	
Item:		Item:	
Date: Amount:		Date: Amount:	
Item:		Item:	
Date: Amount:		Date: Amount:	
Item:		Item:	
Date: Amount:		Date: Amount:	
Item:		Item:	
Number of Items for the Day:		**Total Amount Spent:**	

DAILY SPENDING RECORD
APRIL 2025

Week Start Date: _____ **Week End Date:** _____

Date:	Amount:	Date:	Amount:
Item:		Item:	
Date:	Amount:	Date:	Amount:
Item:		Item:	
Date:	Amount:	Date:	Amount:
Item:		Item:	
Date:	Amount:	Date:	Amount:
Item:		Item:	
Date:	Amount:	Date:	Amount:
Item:		Item:	
Date:	Amount:	Date:	Amount:
Item:		Item:	
Number of Items for the Day:		**Total Amount Spent:**	

DAILY SPENDING RECORD
APRIL 2025

Week Start Date: _____ **Week End Date:** _____

Date:	Amount:	Date:	Amount:
Item:		Item:	
Date:	Amount:	Date:	Amount:
Item:		Item:	
Date:	Amount:	Date:	Amount:
Item:		Item:	
Date:	Amount:	Date:	Amount:
Item:		Item:	
Date:	Amount:	Date:	Amount:
Item:		Item:	
Date:	Amount:	Date:	Amount:
Item:		Item:	
Number of Items for the Day:		**Total Amount Spent:**	

DAILY SPENDING RECORD
APRIL 2025

Week Start Date: _____ **Week End Date:** _____

Date:	Amount:	Date:	Amount:
Item:		Item:	
Date:	Amount:	Date:	Amount:
Item:		Item:	
Date:	Amount:	Date:	Amount:
Item:		Item:	
Date:	Amount:	Date:	Amount:
Item:		Item:	
Date:	Amount:	Date:	Amount:
Item:		Item:	
Date:	Amount:	Date:	Amount:
Item:		Item:	
Number of Items for the Day:		**Total Amount Spent:**	

DAILY SPENDING RECORD
APRIL 2025

Week Start Date: _____ **Week End Date:** _____

Date:	Amount:	Date:	Amount:
Item:		Item:	
Date:	Amount:	Date:	Amount:
Item:		Item:	
Date:	Amount:	Date:	Amount:
Item:		Item:	
Date:	Amount:	Date:	Amount:
Item:		Item:	
Date:	Amount:	Date:	Amount:
Item:		Item:	
Date:	Amount:	Date:	Amount:
Item:		Item:	
Number of Items for the Day:		**Total Amount Spent:**	

Set a goal to make 2025 the year of abundance. Use the form below to track every penny that you're receiving. It's amazing that when your mind is focused on abundance, you begin to create abundance.

DAILY INCOME RECORD
APRIL 2025

	Date	Source	Amount
1			
2			
3			
4			
5			
6			
7			
8			
9			
10			
11			
12			
13			
14			
15			
16			
17			
18			
19			
20			
21			
22			
23			
24			
25			
26			
27			
28			
29			
30			

CULTIVATE AN ATTITUDE OF GRATITUDE

Everyday take 10 to 15 minutes to write down a few things you are grateful for. Don't just write things down really feel what you are writing. The more grateful you are the more financial blessings will come your way. I am speaking from my own experience. Try it, it really works.

1. _____

2. _____

3. _____

4. _____

5. _____

6. _____

7. _____

8. _____

9. _____

10. _____

11. _____

12. _____

13. _____

14. _____

15. _____

16. _____

17. _____

18. _____

19. _____

20 _____

MAY 2025

AFFIRMATION

Today I will make a commitment to act like where I'm going and not where I am at.

Financial Goal for May 2025: _____

_____

SUN	MON	TUE	WED	THU	FRI	SAT
				1	2	3
4	5	6	7	8	9	10
11	12	13	14	15	16	17
18	19	20	21	22	23	24
25	26	27	28	29	30	31

SIX DAILY EMPOWERING QUESTIONS TO BOOST YOUR INCOME

Question 1: Discover Hidden Treasures: Each day, embark on a treasure hunt within your life. Ask yourself: What valuable possessions or assets can I offer for sale today? Share these gems on digital marketplaces and enlist the support of your warm network of friends and family to help you broadcast the news. Their assistance can be the catalyst for spreading the word far and wide.

_____

_____

_____

Question 2: Settle Past Accounts: Revisit your financial history and remind yourself of any outstanding debts owed to you. Reach out to these individuals and ensure that you collect what is rightfully yours.

_____

_____

_____

Question 3: Crafting Value to Share: Explore your artistic side and inquire: What valuable creations can I craft to share with others? Think about crafting handmade goods or offering digital prints as prime examples of how your creativity can translate into financial gains.

_____

_____

_____

_____

Question 4: Unleash Your Skills for Profit: Unleash your inner entrepreneur by pondering the following: What simple services can I provide in exchange for income? Consider your unique abilities, from mowing lawns and providing handyman services to diving into social media marketing, making calls, offering business coaching, consulting services, or administrative wizardry. Capitalize on your talents that have garnered admiration, as they can swiftly translate into a source of cash flow.

_____

_____

_____

Question 5: Solve Problems for Profit: Channel your creativity by asking: What common problems can I effortlessly solve? Identify your exceptional qualifications, talents, and skills that can be harnessed to generate swift income.

_____

_____

_____

Question 6: Trust in Networking: Lastly, consider your network of trustworthy connections. Is there someone you trust, and who trusts you, from whom you can secure a short-term loan if needed? Building on established relationships can provide vital financial support when you need it most.

_____

_____

_____

Your daily engagement with these questions can be a transformative step towards enhancing your financial well-being. Embrace the opportunity to unlock your financial potential!"

UNLOCKING FINANCIAL PROSPERITY THROUGH BUDGETING

Welcome to the path of financial empowerment. To take control of your financial destiny, harness the power of budgeting with the following guidance:

Step 1: Crafting Your Monthly Budget: Begin your journey by utilizing the form provided to create a comprehensive monthly budget. Initiate the process by documenting all your sources of income, leaving no potential revenue stream unaccounted for.

Step 2: Financial Planning: Start by being very clear about what you intend to spend during the course of the month. This includes allocating funds for essential categories such as housing, utilities, groceries, transportation, entertainment, and any other anticipated expenses.

Step 3: Analyzing Real-World Expenditure: At the end of the month, engage in an exercise of tracking your actual spending across various expense categories. This crucial step allows you to ascertain how closely your financial reality aligns with your initial budgetary projections.

Step 4: Prepare for Astonishing Revelations: As you compare your Total Monthly Income against both your Total Monthly Expenses and your Total Actual Spending, you may find yourself astounded. This insightful exercise often unveils a stark contrast between your perception of spending and the fiscal reality you have experienced.

Step 5: Harness the Power of Budgeting: Budgeting serves as a formidable instrument to commandeer your financial destiny. By consistently monitoring your income and expenses, you empower yourself to make informed financial decisions. As a result, you pave the way for building wealth and achieving the financial prosperity you aspire to attain."

MONTHLY INCOME AND EXPENSES WORKSHEET

Monthly Income Per Month

Products   _____ $_____

Services   _____ $_____

Other Income

Bonus $_____

Commission $_____

Grants $_____

Other $_____ $_____

Other $_____ $_____

Total Income $_____

BUDGETING BUILDS WEALTH

Use the form below to create your monthly budget. Start by writing down what you plan to spend for the month. At the end of the month, write in what you actually spent for the month and then compare the two lists. You will be amazed at how much you think you are spending compared to what you are actually have spent.

Monthly Expenses	Budget	Actual
Salary	_____	_____
Mortgage or Rent	_____	_____
Insurance	_____	_____
Appliance Payments	_____	_____
Cable	_____	_____
Taxes	_____	_____
Electricity	_____	_____
Gas	_____	_____
Water	_____	_____
Trash/Recycle/Sewage	_____	_____
Telephone (Office)	_____	_____
Cell Phone	_____	_____
Internet	_____	_____
Office Maintenance	_____	_____
Food (Eating Out)	_____	_____
Automobile Payment	_____	_____

Gas and Oil   _____   _____

Car Insurance   _____   _____

License   _____   _____

Automobile Repairs   _____   _____

Life Insurance   _____   _____

Medical Insurance   _____   _____

Childcare   _____   _____

Savings/Investments   _____   _____

Clothing   _____   _____

Dry Cleaning/Laundry   _____   _____

Printing   _____   _____

Office/Cleaning Supplies   _____   _____

Tuition/Education   _____   _____

Dues/Memberships   _____   _____

Gifts   _____   _____

Apps/Subscriptions   _____   _____

Books and Magazines   _____   _____

Entertainment   _____   _____

Travel   _____   _____

Marketing and Advertising   _____   _____

Total Expenses $_____ $_____

FINANCIAL REALITY TOTAL

Monthly Income $\$$_____

      Subtract

Total Expenses $\$$_____

      Surplus + $\$$_____

      Deficit - $\$$_____

Do you have a surplus or a deficit at the end of the month?

_____Surplus   _____Deficit

If you are spending more than you earn, there are some major changes that need to take place.

How can you increase your income?

1.   6.

2.   7.

3.   8.

4.   9.

5.   10.

How can you cut your spending? What are the items that you can do without?

1.   6.

2.   7.

3.   8.

4.   9.

5.   10.

TRACK YOUR SPENDING

It's very important that you track your spending on this journey. You must be aware of where each and every penny is going. Use the forms below to track your daily spending. The goal is to get rid of wasteful spending and plan for your financial future.

DAILY SPENDING RECORD
MAY 2025

Week Start Date: _____   **Week End Date:** _____

Date: Amount:	Date: Amount:
Item:	Item:
Date: Amount:	Date: Amount:
Item:	Item:
Date: Amount:	Date: Amount:
Item:	Item:
Date: Amount:	Date: Amount:
Item:	Item:
Date: Amount:	Date: Amount:
Item:	Item:
Date: Amount:	Date: Amount:
Item:	Item:
Number of Items for the Day:	**Total Amount Spent:**

DAILY SPENDING RECORD
MAY 2025

Week Start Date: _____ **Week End Date:** _____

Date: Amount: Item:	Date: Amount: Item:
Date: Amount: Item:	Date: Amount: Item:
Date: Amount: Item:	Date: Amount: Item:
Date: Amount: Item:	Date: Amount: Item:
Date: Amount: Item:	Date: Amount: Item:
Date: Amount: Item:	Date: Amount: Item:
Number of Items for the Day:	**Total Amount Spent:**

DAILY SPENDING RECORD
MAY 2025

Week Start Date: _____ **Week End Date:** _____

Date: Amount: Item:	Date: Amount: Item:
Date: Amount: Item:	Date: Amount: Item:
Date: Amount: Item:	Date: Amount: Item:
Date: Amount: Item:	Date: Amount: Item:
Date: Amount: Item:	Date: Amount: Item:
Date: Amount: Item:	Date: Amount: Item:
Number of Items for the Day:	**Total Amount Spent:**

DAILY SPENDING RECORD
MAY 2025

Week Start Date: _____ **Week End Date:** _____

Date: Amount:	Date: Amount:
Item:	Item:
Date: Amount:	Date: Amount:
Item:	Item:
Date: Amount:	Date: Amount:
Item:	Item:
Date: Amount:	Date: Amount:
Item:	Item:
Date: Amount:	Date: Amount:
Item:	Item:
Date: Amount:	Date: Amount:
Item:	Item:
Number of Items for the Day:	**Total Amount Spent:**

DAILY SPENDING RECORD
MAY 2025

Week Start Date: _____ **Week End Date:** _____

Date: Amount:	Date: Amount:
Item:	Item:
Date: Amount:	Date: Amount:
Item:	Item:
Date: Amount:	Date: Amount:
Item:	Item:
Date: Amount:	Date: Amount:
Item:	Item:
Date: Amount:	Date: Amount:
Item:	Item:
Date: Amount:	Date: Amount:
Item:	Item:
Number of Items for the Day:	**Total Amount Spent:**

Set a goal to make 2025 the year of abundance. Use the form below to track every penny that you're receiving. It's amazing that when your mind is focused on abundance, you begin to create abundance.

DAILY INCOME RECORD
MAY 2025

	Date	Source	Amount
1			
2			
3			
4			
5			
6			
7			
8			
9			
10			
11			
12			
13			
14			
15			
16			
17			
18			
19			
20			
21			
22			
23			
24			
25			
26			
27			
28			
29			
30			
31			

CULTIVATE AN ATTITUDE OF GRATITUDE

Everyday take 10 to 15 minutes to write down a few things you are grateful for. Don't just write things down really feel what you are writing. The more grateful you are the more financial blessings will come your way. I am speaking from my own experience. Try it, it really works.

1. _____

2. _____

3. _____

4. _____

5. _____

6. _____

7. _____

8. _____

9. _____

10. _____

11. _____

12. _____

13. _____

14. _____

15. _____

16. _____

17. _____

18. _____

19. _____

20 _____

JUNE 2025

I have a clear vision of what debt-freedom and abundance looks like.

Financial Goal for June 2025: _____

_____

SUN	MON	TUE	WED	THU	FRI	SAT
1	2	3	4	5	6	7
8	9	10	11	12	13	14
15	16	17	18	19	20	21
22	23	24	25	26	27	28
29	30					

SIX DAILY EMPOWERING QUESTIONS TO BOOST YOUR INCOME

Question 1: Discover Hidden Treasures: Each day, embark on a treasure hunt within your life. Ask yourself: What valuable possessions or assets can I offer for sale today? Share these gems on digital marketplaces and enlist the support of your warm network of friends and family to help you broadcast the news. Their assistance can be the catalyst for spreading the word far and wide.

_____

_____

_____

Question 2: Settle Past Accounts: Revisit your financial history and remind yourself of any outstanding debts owed to you. Reach out to these individuals and ensure that you collect what is rightfully yours.

_____

_____

_____

Question 3: Crafting Value to Share: Explore your artistic side and inquire: What valuable creations can I craft to share with others? Think about crafting handmade goods or offering digital prints as prime examples of how your creativity can translate into financial gains.

_____

_____

_____

_____

Question 4: Unleash Your Skills for Profit: Unleash your inner entrepreneur by pondering the following: What simple services can I provide in exchange for income? Consider your unique abilities, from mowing lawns and providing handyman services to diving into social media marketing, making calls, offering business coaching, consulting services, or administrative wizardry. Capitalize on your talents that have garnered admiration, as they can swiftly translate into a source of cash flow.

_____

_____

_____

Question 5: Solve Problems for Profit: Channel your creativity by asking: What common problems can I effortlessly solve? Identify your exceptional qualifications, talents, and skills that can be harnessed to generate swift income.

_____

_____

_____

Question 6: Trust in Networking: Lastly, consider your network of trustworthy connections. Is there someone you trust, and who trusts you, from whom you can secure a short-term loan if needed? Building on established relationships can provide vital financial support when you need it most.

_____

_____

_____

Your daily engagement with these questions can be a transformative step towards enhancing your financial well-being. Embrace the opportunity to unlock your financial potential!"

UNLOCKING FINANCIAL PROSPERITY THROUGH BUDGETING

Welcome to the path of financial empowerment. To take control of your financial destiny, harness the power of budgeting with the following guidance:

Step 1: Crafting Your Monthly Budget: Begin your journey by utilizing the form provided to create a comprehensive monthly budget. Initiate the process by documenting all your sources of income, leaving no potential revenue stream unaccounted for.

Step 2: Financial Planning: Start by being very clear about what you intend to spend during the course of the month. This includes allocating funds for essential categories such as housing, utilities, groceries, transportation, entertainment, and any other anticipated expenses.

Step 3: Analyzing Real-World Expenditure: At the end of the month, engage in an exercise of tracking your actual spending across various expense categories. This crucial step allows you to ascertain how closely your financial reality aligns with your initial budgetary projections.

Step 4: Prepare for Astonishing Revelations: As you compare your Total Monthly Income against both your Total Monthly Expenses and your Total Actual Spending, you may find yourself astounded. This insightful exercise often unveils a stark contrast between your perception of spending and the fiscal reality you have experienced.

Step 5: Harness the Power of Budgeting: Budgeting serves as a formidable instrument to commandeer your financial destiny. By consistently monitoring your income and expenses, you empower yourself to make informed financial decisions. As a result, you pave the way for building wealth and achieving the financial prosperity you aspire to attain."

MONTHLY INCOME AND EXPENSES WORKSHEET

Monthly Income Per Month

Products   _____ $_____

Services   _____ $_____

Other Income

Bonus $_____

Commission $_____

Grants $_____

Other $_____ $_____

Other $_____ $_____

Total Income $_____

BUDGETING BUILDS WEALTH

Use the form below to create your monthly budget. Start by writing down what you plan to spend for the month. At the end of the month, write in what you actually spent for the month and then compare the two lists. You will be amazed at how much you think you are spending compared to what you are actually have spent.

Monthly Expenses	Budget	Actual
Salary	_____	_____
Mortgage or Rent	_____	_____
Insurance	_____	_____
Appliance Payments	_____	_____
Cable	_____	_____
Taxes	_____	_____
Electricity	_____	_____
Gas	_____	_____
Water	_____	_____
Trash/Recycle/Sewage	_____	_____
Telephone (Office)	_____	_____
Cell Phone	_____	_____
Internet	_____	_____
Office Maintenance	_____	_____
Food (Eating Out)	_____	_____
Automobile Payment	_____	_____

Gas and Oil	_____	_____
Car Insurance	_____	_____
License	_____	_____
Automobile Repairs	_____	_____
Life Insurance	_____	_____
Medical Insurance	_____	_____
Childcare	_____	_____
Savings/Investments	_____	_____
Clothing	_____	_____
Dry Cleaning/Laundry	_____	_____
Printing	_____	_____
Office/Cleaning Supplies	_____	_____
Tuition/Education	_____	_____
Dues/Memberships	_____	_____
Gifts	_____	_____
Apps/Subscriptions	_____	_____
Books and Magazines	_____	_____
Entertainment	_____	_____
Travel	_____	_____
Marketing and Advertising	_____	_____
Total Expenses	$_____	$_____

FINANCIAL REALITY TOTAL

Monthly Income $_____

      Subtract

Total Expenses $_____

      Surplus + $_____

      Deficit - $_____

Do you have a surplus or a deficit at the end of the month?

_____Surplus   _____Deficit

If you are spending more than you earn, there are some major changes that need to take place.

How can you increase your income?

1.   6.

2.   7.

3.   8.

4.   9.

5.   10.

How can you cut your spending? What are the items that you can do without?

1.   6.

2.   7.

3.   8.

4.   9.

5.   10.

TRACK YOUR SPENDING

It's very important that you track your spending on this journey. You must be aware of where each and every penny is going. Use the forms below to track your daily spending. The goal is to get rid of wasteful spending and plan for your financial future.

DAILY SPENDING RECORD
JUNE 2025

Week Start Date: _____ **Week End Date:** _____

Date: Amount:	Date: Amount:
Item:	Item:
Date: Amount:	Date: Amount:
Item:	Item:
Date: Amount:	Date: Amount:
Item:	Item:
Date: Amount:	Date: Amount:
Item:	Item:
Date: Amount:	Date: Amount:
Item:	Item:
Date: Amount:	Date: Amount:
Item:	Item:
Number of Items for the Day:	**Total Amount Spent:**

DAILY SPENDING RECORD
JUNE 2025

Week Start Date: _____   **Week End Date:** _____

Date: Amount: Item:	Date: Amount: Item:
Date: Amount: Item:	Date: Amount: Item:
Date: Amount: Item:	Date: Amount: Item:
Date: Amount: Item:	Date: Amount: Item:
Date: Amount: Item:	Date: Amount: Item:
Date: Amount: Item:	Date: Amount: Item:
Number of Items for the Day:	**Total Amount Spent:**

DAILY SPENDING RECORD
JUNE 2025

Week Start Date: _____   **Week End Date:** _____

Date: Amount: Item:	Date: Amount: Item:
Date: Amount: Item:	Date: Amount: Item:
Date: Amount: Item:	Date: Amount: Item:
Date: Amount: Item:	Date: Amount: Item:
Date: Amount: Item:	Date: Amount: Item:
Date: Amount: Item:	Date: Amount: Item:
Number of Items for the Day:	**Total Amount Spent:**

DAILY SPENDING RECORD
JUNE 2025

Week Start Date: _____ **Week End Date:** _____

Date: Amount: Item:	Date: Amount: Item:
Date: Amount: Item:	Date: Amount: Item:
Date: Amount: Item:	Date: Amount: Item:
Date: Amount: Item:	Date: Amount: Item:
Date: Amount: Item:	Date: Amount: Item:
Date: Amount: Item:	Date: Amount: Item:
Number of Items for the Day:	**Total Amount Spent:**

DAILY SPENDING RECORD
JUNE 2025

Week Start Date: _____ **Week End Date:** _____

Date: Amount: Item:	Date: Amount: Item:
Date: Amount: Item:	Date: Amount: Item:
Date: Amount: Item:	Date: Amount: Item:
Date: Amount: Item:	Date: Amount: Item:
Date: Amount: Item:	Date: Amount: Item:
Date: Amount: Item:	Date: Amount: Item:
Number of Items for the Day:	**Total Amount Spent:**

Set a goal to make 2025 the year of abundance. Use the form below to track every penny that you're receiving. It's amazing that when your mind is focused on abundance, you begin to create abundance.

DAILY INCOME RECORD
JUNE 2025

	Date	Source	Amount
1			
2			
3			
4			
5			
6			
7			
8			
9			
10			
11			
12			
13			
14			
15			
16			
17			
18			
19			
20			
21			
22			
23			
24			
25			
26			
27			
28			
29			
30			

CULTIVATE AN ATTITUDE OF GRATITUDE

Everyday take 10 to 15 minutes to write down a few things you are grateful for. Don't just write things down really feel what you are writing. The more grateful you are the more financial blessings will come your way. I am speaking from my own experience. Try it, it really works.

1. _____
2. _____
3. _____
4. _____
5. _____
6. _____
7. _____
8. _____
9. _____
10. _____
11. _____
12. _____
13. _____
14. _____
15. _____
16. _____
17. _____
18. _____
19. _____
20 _____

JULY 2025

Financial Goal for July 2025: _____

_____

SUN	MON	TUE	WED	THU	FRI	SAT
		1	2	3	4	5
6	7	8	9	10	11	12
13	14	15	16	17	18	19
20	21	22	23	24	25	26
27	28	29	30	31		

SIX DAILY EMPOWERING QUESTIONS TO BOOST YOUR INCOME

Question 1: Discover Hidden Treasures: Each day, embark on a treasure hunt within your life. Ask yourself: What valuable possessions or assets can I offer for sale today? Share these gems on digital marketplaces and enlist the support of your warm network of friends and family to help you broadcast the news. Their assistance can be the catalyst for spreading the word far and wide.

_____

_____

_____

Question 2: Settle Past Accounts: Revisit your financial history and remind yourself of any outstanding debts owed to you. Reach out to these individuals and ensure that you collect what is rightfully yours.

_____

_____

_____

Question 3: Crafting Value to Share: Explore your artistic side and inquire: What valuable creations can I craft to share with others? Think about crafting handmade goods or offering digital prints as prime examples of how your creativity can translate into financial gains.

_____

_____

_____

_____

Question 4: Unleash Your Skills for Profit: Unleash your inner entrepreneur by pondering the following: What simple services can I provide in exchange for income? Consider your unique abilities, from mowing lawns and providing handyman services to diving into social media marketing, making calls, offering business coaching, consulting services, or administrative wizardry. Capitalize on your talents that have garnered admiration, as they can swiftly translate into a source of cash flow.

_____

_____

_____

Question 5: Solve Problems for Profit: Channel your creativity by asking: What common problems can I effortlessly solve? Identify your exceptional qualifications, talents, and skills that can be harnessed to generate swift income.

_____

_____

_____

Question 6: Trust in Networking: Lastly, consider your network of trustworthy connections. Is there someone you trust, and who trusts you, from whom you can secure a short-term loan if needed? Building on established relationships can provide vital financial support when you need it most.

_____

_____

_____

Your daily engagement with these questions can be a transformative step towards enhancing your financial well-being. Embrace the opportunity to unlock your financial potential!"

UNLOCKING FINANCIAL PROSPERITY THROUGH BUDGETING

Welcome to the path of financial empowerment. To take control of your financial destiny, harness the power of budgeting with the following guidance:

Step 1: Crafting Your Monthly Budget: Begin your journey by utilizing the form provided to create a comprehensive monthly budget. Initiate the process by documenting all your sources of income, leaving no potential revenue stream unaccounted for.

Step 2: Financial Planning: Start by being very clear about what you intend to spend during the course of the month. This includes allocating funds for essential categories such as housing, utilities, groceries, transportation, entertainment, and any other anticipated expenses.

Step 3: Analyzing Real-World Expenditure: At the end of the month, engage in an exercise of tracking your actual spending across various expense categories. This crucial step allows you to ascertain how closely your financial reality aligns with your initial budgetary projections.

Step 4: Prepare for Astonishing Revelations: As you compare your Total Monthly Income against both your Total Monthly Expenses and your Total Actual Spending, you may find yourself astounded. This insightful exercise often unveils a stark contrast between your perception of spending and the fiscal reality you have experienced.

Step 5: Harness the Power of Budgeting: Budgeting serves as a formidable instrument to commandeer your financial destiny. By consistently monitoring your income and expenses, you empower yourself to make informed financial decisions. As a result, you pave the way for building wealth and achieving the financial prosperity you aspire to attain."

MONTHLY INCOME AND EXPENSES WORKSHEET

Monthly Income Per Month

Products	_____	$_____
Services	_____	$_____

Other Income

Bonus		$_____
Commission		$_____
Grants		$_____
Other	$_____	$_____
Other	$_____	$_____

Total Income $_____

BUDGETING BUILDS WEALTH

Use the form below to create your monthly budget. Start by writing down what you plan to spend for the month. At the end of the month, write in what you actually spent for the month and then compare the two lists. You will be amazed at how much you think you are spending compared to what you are actually have spent.

Monthly Expenses	Budget	Actual
Salary	_____	_____
Mortgage or Rent	_____	_____
Insurance	_____	_____
Appliance Payments	_____	_____
Cable	_____	_____
Taxes	_____	_____
Electricity	_____	_____
Gas	_____	_____
Water	_____	_____
Trash/Recycle/Sewage	_____	_____
Telephone (Office)	_____	_____
Cell Phone	_____	_____
Internet	_____	_____
Office Maintenance	_____	_____
Food (Eating Out)	_____	_____
Automobile Payment	_____	_____

Gas and Oil   _____   _____

Car Insurance   _____   _____

License   _____   _____

Automobile Repairs   _____   _____

Life Insurance   _____   _____

Medical Insurance   _____   _____

Childcare   _____   _____

Savings/Investments   _____   _____

Clothing   _____   _____

Dry Cleaning/Laundry   _____   _____

Printing   _____   _____

Office/Cleaning Supplies   _____   _____

Tuition/Education   _____   _____

Dues/Memberships   _____   _____

Gifts   _____   _____

Apps/Subscriptions   _____   _____

Books and Magazines   _____   _____

Entertainment   _____   _____

Travel   _____   _____

Marketing and Advertising   _____   _____

Total Expenses $_____ $_____

FINANCIAL REALITY TOTAL

Monthly Income $_____

      Subtract

Total Expenses $_____

      Surplus + $_____

      Deficit - $_____

Do you have a surplus or a deficit at the end of the month?

_____Surplus   _____Deficit

If you are spending more than you earn, there are some major changes that need to take place.

How can you increase your income?

1.   6.

2.   7.

3.   8.

4.   9.

5.   10.

How can you cut your spending? What are the items that you can do without?

1.   6.

2.   7.

3.   8.

4.   9.

5.   10.

TRACK YOUR SPENDING

It's very important that you track your spending on this journey. You must be aware of where each and every penny is going. Use the forms below to track your daily spending. The goal is to get rid of wasteful spending and plan for your financial future.

DAILY SPENDING RECORD
JULY 2025

Week Start Date: _____ **Week End Date:** _____

Date: Amount: Item:	Date: Amount: Item:	
Date: Amount: Item:	Date: Amount: Item:	
Date: Amount: Item:	Date: Amount: Item:	
Date: Amount: Item:	Date: Amount: Item:	
Date: Amount: Item:	Date: Amount: Item:	
Date: Amount: Item:	Date: Amount: Item:	
Number of Items for the Day:	**Total Amount Spent:**	

DAILY SPENDING RECORD
JULY 2025

Week Start Date: _____   **Week End Date:** _____

Date: Amount: Item:	Date: Amount: Item:
Date: Amount: Item:	Date: Amount: Item:
Date: Amount: Item:	Date: Amount: Item:
Date: Amount: Item:	Date: Amount: Item:
Date: Amount: Item:	Date: Amount: Item:
Date: Amount: Item:	Date: Amount: Item:
Number of Items for the Day:	**Total Amount Spent:**

DAILY SPENDING RECORD
JULY 2025

Week Start Date: _____   **Week End Date:** _____

Date: Amount: Item:	Date: Amount: Item:
Date: Amount: Item:	Date: Amount: Item:
Date: Amount: Item:	Date: Amount: Item:
Date: Amount: Item:	Date: Amount: Item:
Date: Amount: Item:	Date: Amount: Item:
Date: Amount: Item:	Date: Amount: Item:
Number of Items for the Day:	**Total Amount Spent:**

DAILY SPENDING RECORD
JULY 2025

Week Start Date: _____ **Week End Date:** _____

Date: Amount: Item:	Date: Amount: Item:
Date: Amount: Item:	Date: Amount: Item:
Date: Amount: Item:	Date: Amount: Item:
Date: Amount: Item:	Date: Amount: Item:
Date: Amount: Item:	Date: Amount: Item:
Date: Amount: Item:	Date: Amount: Item:
Number of Items for the Day:	**Total Amount Spent:**

DAILY SPENDING RECORD
JULY 2025

Week Start Date: _____ **Week End Date:** _____

Date: Amount: Item:	Date: Amount: Item:
Date: Amount: Item:	Date: Amount: Item:
Date: Amount: Item:	Date: Amount: Item:
Date: Amount: Item:	Date: Amount: Item:
Date: Amount: Item:	Date: Amount: Item:
Date: Amount: Item:	Date: Amount: Item:
Number of Items for the Day:	**Total Amount Spent:**

Set a goal to make 2025 the year of abundance. Use the form below to track every penny that you're receiving. It's amazing that when your mind is focused on abundance, you begin to create abundance.

DAILY INCOME RECORD
JULY 2025

	Date	Source	Amount
1			
2			
3			
4			
5			
6			
7			
8			
9			
10			
11			
12			
13			
14			
15			
16			
17			
18			
19			
20			
21			
22			
23			
24			
25			
26			
27			
28			
29			
30			
31			

CULTIVATE AN ATTITUDE OF GRATITUDE

Everyday take 10 to 15 minutes to write down a few things you are grateful for. Don't just write things down really feel what you are writing. The more grateful you are the more financial blessings will come your way. I am speaking from my own experience. Try it, it really works.

1. _____
2. _____
3. _____
4. _____
5. _____
6. _____
7. _____
8. _____
9. _____
10. _____
11. _____
12. _____
13. _____
14. _____
15. _____
16. _____
17. _____
18. _____
19. _____
20 _____

AUGUST 2025

Financial Goal for August 2025: _____

_____

SUN	MON	TUE	WED	THU	FRI	SAT
					1	2
3	4	5	6	7	8	9
10	11	12	13	14	15	16
17	18	19	20	21	22	23
24	25	26	27	28	29	30
31						

SIX DAILY EMPOWERING QUESTIONS TO BOOST YOUR INCOME

Question 1: Discover Hidden Treasures: Each day, embark on a treasure hunt within your life. Ask yourself: What valuable possessions or assets can I offer for sale today? Share these gems on digital marketplaces and enlist the support of your warm network of friends and family to help you broadcast the news. Their assistance can be the catalyst for spreading the word far and wide.

_____

_____

_____

Question 2: Settle Past Accounts: Revisit your financial history and remind yourself of any outstanding debts owed to you. Reach out to these individuals and ensure that you collect what is rightfully yours.

_____

_____

_____

Question 3: Crafting Value to Share: Explore your artistic side and inquire: What valuable creations can I craft to share with others? Think about crafting handmade goods or offering digital prints as prime examples of how your creativity can translate into financial gains.

_____

_____

_____

_____

Question 4: Unleash Your Skills for Profit: Unleash your inner entrepreneur by pondering the following: What simple services can I provide in exchange for income? Consider your unique abilities, from mowing lawns and providing handyman services to diving into social media marketing, making calls, offering business coaching, consulting services, or administrative wizardry. Capitalize on your talents that have garnered admiration, as they can swiftly translate into a source of cash flow.

_____

_____

_____

Question 5: Solve Problems for Profit: Channel your creativity by asking: What common problems can I effortlessly solve? Identify your exceptional qualifications, talents, and skills that can be harnessed to generate swift income.

_____

_____

_____

Question 6: Trust in Networking: Lastly, consider your network of trustworthy connections. Is there someone you trust, and who trusts you, from whom you can secure a short-term loan if needed? Building on established relationships can provide vital financial support when you need it most.

_____

_____

_____

Your daily engagement with these questions can be a transformative step towards enhancing your financial well-being. Embrace the opportunity to unlock your financial potential!"

UNLOCKING FINANCIAL PROSPERITY THROUGH BUDGETING

Welcome to the path of financial empowerment. To take control of your financial destiny, harness the power of budgeting with the following guidance:

Step 1: Crafting Your Monthly Budget: Begin your journey by utilizing the form provided to create a comprehensive monthly budget. Initiate the process by documenting all your sources of income, leaving no potential revenue stream unaccounted for.

Step 2: Financial Planning: Start by being very clear about what you intend to spend during the course of the month. This includes allocating funds for essential categories such as housing, utilities, groceries, transportation, entertainment, and any other anticipated expenses.

Step 3: Analyzing Real-World Expenditure: At the end of the month, engage in an exercise of tracking your actual spending across various expense categories. This crucial step allows you to ascertain how closely your financial reality aligns with your initial budgetary projections.

Step 4: Prepare for Astonishing Revelations: As you compare your Total Monthly Income against both your Total Monthly Expenses and your Total Actual Spending, you may find yourself astounded. This insightful exercise often unveils a stark contrast between your perception of spending and the fiscal reality you have experienced.

Step 5: Harness the Power of Budgeting: Budgeting serves as a formidable instrument to commandeer your financial destiny. By consistently monitoring your income and expenses, you empower yourself to make informed financial decisions. As a result, you pave the way for building wealth and achieving the financial prosperity you aspire to attain."

MONTHLY INCOME AND EXPENSES WORKSHEET

Monthly Income Per Month

Products   _____ $_____

Services   _____ $_____

Other Income

Bonus $_____

Commission $_____

Grants $_____

Other $_____ $_____

Other $_____ $_____

Total Income $_____

BUDGETING BUILDS WEALTH

Use the form below to create your monthly budget. Start by writing down what you plan to spend for the month. At the end of the month, write in what you actually spent for the month and then compare the two lists. You will be amazed at how much you think you are spending compared to what you are actually have spent.

Monthly Expenses	Budget	Actual
Salary	_____	_____
Mortgage or Rent	_____	_____
Insurance	_____	_____
Appliance Payments	_____	_____
Cable	_____	_____
Taxes	_____	_____
Electricity	_____	_____
Gas	_____	_____
Water	_____	_____
Trash/Recycle/Sewage	_____	_____
Telephone (Office)	_____	_____
Cell Phone	_____	_____
Internet	_____	_____
Office Maintenance	_____	_____
Food (Eating Out)	_____	_____
Automobile Payment	_____	_____

Gas and Oil _____ _____

Car Insurance _____ _____

License _____ _____

Automobile Repairs _____ _____

Life Insurance _____ _____

Medical Insurance _____ _____

Childcare _____ _____

Savings/Investments _____ _____

Clothing _____ _____

Dry Cleaning/Laundry _____ _____

Printing _____ _____

Office/Cleaning Supplies _____ _____

Tuition/Education _____ _____

Dues/Memberships _____ _____

Gifts _____ _____

Apps/Subscriptions _____ _____

Books and Magazines _____ _____

Entertainment _____ _____

Travel _____ _____

Marketing and Advertising _____ _____

Total Expenses $_____ $_____

FINANCIAL REALITY TOTAL

Monthly Income $_____

      Subtract

Total Expenses $_____

      Surplus + $_____

      Deficit - $_____

Do you have a surplus or a deficit at the end of the month?

_____Surplus   _____Deficit

If you are spending more than you earn, there are some major changes that need to take place.

How can you increase your income?

1.   6.

2.   7.

3.   8.

4.   9.

5.   10.

How can you cut your spending? What are the items that you can do without?

1.   6.

2.   7.

3.   8.

4.   9.

5.   10.

TRACK YOUR SPENDING

It's very important that you track your spending on this journey. You must be aware of where each and every penny is going. Use the forms below to track your daily spending. The goal is to get rid of wasteful spending and plan for your financial future.

DAILY SPENDING RECORD
AUGUST 2025

Week Start Date: _____   **Week End Date:** _____

Date:	Amount:	Date:	Amount:
Item:		Item:	
Date:	Amount:	Date:	Amount:
Item:		Item:	
Date:	Amount:	Date:	Amount:
Item:		Item:	
Date:	Amount:	Date:	Amount:
Item:		Item:	
Date:	Amount:	Date:	Amount:
Item:		Item:	
Date:	Amount:	Date:	Amount:
Item:		Item:	
Number of Items for the Day:		**Total Amount Spent:**	

DAILY SPENDING RECORD
AUGUST 2025

Week Start Date: _____   **Week End Date:** _____

Date: Amount:	Date: Amount:
Item:	Item:
Date: Amount:	Date: Amount:
Item:	Item:
Date: Amount:	Date: Amount:
Item:	Item:
Date: Amount:	Date: Amount:
Item:	Item:
Date: Amount:	Date: Amount:
Item:	Item:
Date: Amount:	Date: Amount:
Item:	Item:
Number of Items for the Day:	**Total Amount Spent:**

DAILY SPENDING RECORD
AUGUST 2025

Week Start Date: _____   **Week End Date:** _____

Date: Amount:	Date: Amount:
Item:	Item:
Date: Amount:	Date: Amount:
Item:	Item:
Date: Amount:	Date: Amount:
Item:	Item:
Date: Amount:	Date: Amount:
Item:	Item:
Date: Amount:	Date: Amount:
Item:	Item:
Date: Amount:	Date: Amount:
Item:	Item:
Number of Items for the Day:	**Total Amount Spent:**

DAILY SPENDING RECORD
AUGUST 2025

Week Start Date: _____ **Week End Date:** _____

Date: Amount: Item:	Date: Amount: Item:
Date: Amount: Item:	Date: Amount: Item:
Date: Amount: Item:	Date: Amount: Item:
Date: Amount: Item:	Date: Amount: Item:
Date: Amount: Item:	Date: Amount: Item:
Date: Amount: Item:	Date: Amount: Item:
Number of Items for the Day:	**Total Amount Spent:**

DAILY SPENDING RECORD
AUGUST 2025

Week Start Date: _____ **Week End Date:** _____

Date: Amount: Item:	Date: Amount: Item:
Date: Amount: Item:	Date: Amount: Item:
Date: Amount: Item:	Date: Amount: Item:
Date: Amount: Item:	Date: Amount: Item:
Date: Amount: Item:	Date: Amount: Item:
Date: Amount: Item:	Date: Amount: Item:
Number of Items for the Day:	**Total Amount Spent:**

Set a goal to make 2025 the year of abundance. Use the form below to track every penny that you're receiving. It's amazing that when your mind is focused on abundance, you begin to create abundance.

DAILY INCOME RECORD
AUGUST 2025

	Date	Source	Amount
1			
2			
3			
4			
5			
6			
7			
8			
9			
10			
11			
12			
13			
14			
15			
16			
17			
18			
19			
20			
21			
22			
23			
24			
25			
26			
27			
28			
29			
30			
31			

CULTIVATE AN ATTITUDE OF GRATITUDE

Everyday take 10 to 15 minutes to write down a few things you are grateful for. Don't just write things down really feel what you are writing. The more grateful you are the more financial blessings will come your way. I am speaking from my own experience. Try it, it really works.

1. _____
2. _____
3. _____
4. _____
5. _____
6. _____
7. _____
8. _____
9. _____
10. _____
11. _____
12. _____
13. _____
14. _____
15. _____
16. _____
17. _____
18. _____
19. _____
20 _____

SEPTEMBER 2025

Financial Goal for September 2025: _____

SUN	MON	TUE	WED	THU	FRI	SAT
		1	2	3	4	5	6
7	8	9	10	11	12	13
14	15	16	17	18	19	20
21	22	23	24	25	26	27
28	29	30				

SIX DAILY EMPOWERING QUESTIONS TO BOOST YOUR INCOME

Question 1: Discover Hidden Treasures: Each day, embark on a treasure hunt within your life. Ask yourself: What valuable possessions or assets can I offer for sale today? Share these gems on digital marketplaces and enlist the support of your warm network of friends and family to help you broadcast the news. Their assistance can be the catalyst for spreading the word far and wide.

Question 2: Settle Past Accounts: Revisit your financial history and remind yourself of any outstanding debts owed to you. Reach out to these individuals and ensure that you collect what is rightfully yours.

Question 3: Crafting Value to Share: Explore your artistic side and inquire: What valuable creations can I craft to share with others? Think about crafting handmade goods or offering digital prints as prime examples of how your creativity can translate into financial gains.

Question 4: Unleash Your Skills for Profit: Unleash your inner entrepreneur by pondering the following: What simple services can I provide in exchange for income? Consider your unique abilities, from mowing lawns and providing handyman services to diving into social media marketing, making calls, offering business coaching, consulting services, or administrative wizardry. Capitalize on your talents that have garnered admiration, as they can swiftly translate into a source of cash flow.

_____

_____

_____

Question 5: Solve Problems for Profit: Channel your creativity by asking: What common problems can I effortlessly solve? Identify your exceptional qualifications, talents, and skills that can be harnessed to generate swift income.

_____

_____

_____

Question 6: Trust in Networking: Lastly, consider your network of trustworthy connections. Is there someone you trust, and who trusts you, from whom you can secure a short-term loan if needed? Building on established relationships can provide vital financial support when you need it most.

_____

_____

_____

Your daily engagement with these questions can be a transformative step towards enhancing your financial well-being. Embrace the opportunity to unlock your financial potential!"

UNLOCKING FINANCIAL PROSPERITY THROUGH BUDGETING

Welcome to the path of financial empowerment. To take control of your financial destiny, harness the power of budgeting with the following guidance:

Step 1: Crafting Your Monthly Budget: Begin your journey by utilizing the form provided to create a comprehensive monthly budget. Initiate the process by documenting all your sources of income, leaving no potential revenue stream unaccounted for.

Step 2: Financial Planning: Start by being very clear about what you intend to spend during the course of the month. This includes allocating funds for essential categories such as housing, utilities, groceries, transportation, entertainment, and any other anticipated expenses.

Step 3: Analyzing Real-World Expenditure: At the end of the month, engage in an exercise of tracking your actual spending across various expense categories. This crucial step allows you to ascertain how closely your financial reality aligns with your initial budgetary projections.

Step 4: Prepare for Astonishing Revelations: As you compare your Total Monthly Income against both your Total Monthly Expenses and your Total Actual Spending, you may find yourself astounded. This insightful exercise often unveils a stark contrast between your perception of spending and the fiscal reality you have experienced.

Step 5: Harness the Power of Budgeting: Budgeting serves as a formidable instrument to commandeer your financial destiny. By consistently monitoring your income and expenses, you empower yourself to make informed financial decisions. As a result, you pave the way for building wealth and achieving the financial prosperity you aspire to attain."

MONTHLY INCOME AND EXPENSES WORKSHEET

Monthly Income Per Month

Products	_____	$_____
Services	_____	$_____

Other Income

Bonus		$_____
Commission		$_____
Grants		$_____
Other	$_____	$_____
Other	$_____	$_____

Total Income $_____

BUDGETING BUILDS WEALTH

Use the form below to create your monthly budget. Start by writing down what you plan to spend for the month. At the end of the month, write in what you actually spent for the month and then compare the two lists. You will be amazed at how much you think you are spending compared to what you are actually have spent.

Monthly Expenses	Budget	Actual
Salary	_____	_____
Mortgage or Rent	_____	_____
Insurance	_____	_____
Appliance Payments	_____	_____
Cable	_____	_____
Taxes	_____	_____
Electricity	_____	_____
Gas	_____	_____
Water	_____	_____
Trash/Recycle/Sewage	_____	_____
Telephone (Office)	_____	_____
Cell Phone	_____	_____
Internet	_____	_____
Office Maintenance	_____	_____
Food (Eating Out)	_____	_____
Automobile Payment	_____	_____

Gas and Oil	_____	_____
Car Insurance	_____	_____
License	_____	_____
Automobile Repairs	_____	_____
Life Insurance	_____	_____
Medical Insurance	_____	_____
Childcare	_____	_____
Savings/Investments	_____	_____
Clothing	_____	_____
Dry Cleaning/Laundry	_____	_____
Printing	_____	_____
Office/Cleaning Supplies	_____	_____
Tuition/Education	_____	_____
Dues/Memberships	_____	_____
Gifts	_____	_____
Apps/Subscriptions	_____	_____
Books and Magazines	_____	_____
Entertainment	_____	_____
Travel	_____	_____
Marketing and Advertising	_____	_____
Total Expenses	$_____	$_____

FINANCIAL REALITY TOTAL

Monthly Income $_____

Subtract
Total Expenses $_____
  Surplus + $_____
  Deficit - $_____

Do you have a surplus or a deficit at the end of the month?
_____Surplus   _____Deficit

If you are spending more than you earn, there are some major changes that need to take place.

How can you increase your income?

1.   6.

2.   7.

3.   8.

4.   9.

5.   10.

How can you cut your spending? What are the items that you can do without?

1.   6.

2.   7.

3.   8.

4.   9.

5.   10.

TRACK YOUR SPENDING

It's very important that you track your spending on this journey. You must be aware of where each and every penny is going. Use the forms below to track your daily spending. The goal is to get rid of wasteful spending and plan for your financial future.

DAILY SPENDING RECORD
SEPTEMBER 2025

Week Start Date: _____   **Week End Date:** _____

Date: Amount: Item:		Date: Amount: Item:	
Date: Amount: Item:		Date: Amount: Item:	
Date: Amount: Item:		Date: Amount: Item:	
Date: Amount: Item:		Date: Amount: Item:	
Date: Amount: Item:		Date: Amount: Item:	
Date: Amount: Item:		Date: Amount: Item:	
Number of Items for the Day:		**Total Amount Spent:**	

DAILY SPENDING RECORD
SEPTEMBER 2025

Week Start Date: _____   **Week End Date:** _____

Date:	Amount:	Date:	Amount:
Item:		Item:	
Date:	Amount:	Date:	Amount:
Item:		Item:	
Date:	Amount:	Date:	Amount:
Item:		Item:	
Date:	Amount:	Date:	Amount:
Item:		Item:	
Date:	Amount:	Date:	Amount:
Item:		Item:	
Date:	Amount:	Date:	Amount:
Item:		Item:	
Number of Items for the Day:		**Total Amount Spent:**	

DAILY SPENDING RECORD
SEPTEMBER 2025

Week Start Date: _____   **Week End Date:** _____

Date:	Amount:	Date:	Amount:
Item:		Item:	
Date:	Amount:	Date:	Amount:
Item:		Item:	
Date:	Amount:	Date:	Amount:
Item:		Item:	
Date:	Amount:	Date:	Amount:
Item:		Item:	
Date:	Amount:	Date:	Amount:
Item:		Item:	
Date:	Amount:	Date:	Amount:
Item:		Item:	
Number of Items for the Day:		**Total Amount Spent:**	

DAILY SPENDING RECORD
SEPTEMBER 2025

Week Start Date: _____ **Week End Date:** _____

Date: Amount: Item:	Date: Amount: Item:
Date: Amount: Item:	Date: Amount: Item:
Date: Amount: Item:	Date: Amount: Item:
Date: Amount: Item:	Date: Amount: Item:
Date: Amount: Item:	Date: Amount: Item:
Date: Amount: Item:	Date: Amount: Item:
Number of Items for the Day:	**Total Amount Spent:**

DAILY SPENDING RECORD
SEPTEMBER 2025

Week Start Date: _____ **Week End Date:** _____

Date: Amount: Item:	Date: Amount: Item:
Date: Amount: Item:	Date: Amount: Item:
Date: Amount: Item:	Date: Amount: Item:
Date: Amount: Item:	Date: Amount: Item:
Date: Amount: Item:	Date: Amount: Item:
Date: Amount: Item:	Date: Amount: Item:
Number of Items for the Day:	**Total Amount Spent:**

Set a goal to make 2025 the year of abundance. Use the form below to track every penny that you're receiving. It's amazing that when your mind is focused on abundance, you begin to create abundance.

DAILY INCOME RECORD
SEPTEMBER 2025

	Date	Source	Amount
1			
2			
3			
4			
5			
6			
7			
8			
9			
10			
11			
12			
13			
14			
15			
16			
17			
18			
19			
20			
21			
22			
23			
24			
25			
26			
27			
28			
29			
30			

CULTIVATE AN ATTITUDE OF GRATITUDE

Everyday take 10 to 15 minutes to write down a few things you are grateful for. Don't just write things down really feel what you are writing. The more grateful you are the more financial blessings will come your way. I am speaking from my own experience. Try it, it really works.

1. _____

2. _____

3. _____

4. _____

5. _____

6. _____

7. _____

8. _____

9. _____

10. _____

11. _____

12. _____

13. _____

14. _____

15. _____

16. _____

17. _____

18. _____

19. _____

20 _____

OCTOBER 2025

Financial Goal for October 2025: _____

SUN	MON	TUE	WED	THU	FRI	SAT
			1	2	3	4
5	6	7	8	9	10	11
12	13	14	15	16	17	18
19	20	21	22	23	24	25
26	27	28	29	30	31	

SIX DAILY EMPOWERING QUESTIONS TO BOOST YOUR INCOME

Question 1: Discover Hidden Treasures: Each day, embark on a treasure hunt within your life. Ask yourself: What valuable possessions or assets can I offer for sale today? Share these gems on digital marketplaces and enlist the support of your warm network of friends and family to help you broadcast the news. Their assistance can be the catalyst for spreading the word far and wide.

_____

_____

_____

Question 2: Settle Past Accounts: Revisit your financial history and remind yourself of any outstanding debts owed to you. Reach out to these individuals and ensure that you collect what is rightfully yours.

_____

_____

_____

Question 3: Crafting Value to Share: Explore your artistic side and inquire: What valuable creations can I craft to share with others? Think about crafting handmade goods or offering digital prints as prime examples of how your creativity can translate into financial gains.

_____

_____

_____

_____

Question 4: Unleash Your Skills for Profit: Unleash your inner entrepreneur by pondering the following: What simple services can I provide in exchange for income? Consider your unique abilities, from mowing lawns and providing handyman services to diving into social media marketing, making calls, offering business coaching, consulting services, or administrative wizardry. Capitalize on your talents that have garnered admiration, as they can swiftly translate into a source of cash flow.

_____

_____

_____

Question 5: Solve Problems for Profit: Channel your creativity by asking: What common problems can I effortlessly solve? Identify your exceptional qualifications, talents, and skills that can be harnessed to generate swift income.

_____

_____

_____

Question 6: Trust in Networking: Lastly, consider your network of trustworthy connections. Is there someone you trust, and who trusts you, from whom you can secure a short-term loan if needed? Building on established relationships can provide vital financial support when you need it most.

_____

_____

_____

Your daily engagement with these questions can be a transformative step towards enhancing your financial well-being. Embrace the opportunity to unlock your financial potential!"

UNLOCKING FINANCIAL PROSPERITY THROUGH BUDGETING

Welcome to the path of financial empowerment. To take control of your financial destiny, harness the power of budgeting with the following guidance:

Step 1: Crafting Your Monthly Budget: Begin your journey by utilizing the form provided to create a comprehensive monthly budget. Initiate the process by documenting all your sources of income, leaving no potential revenue stream unaccounted for.

Step 2: Financial Planning: Start by being very clear about what you intend to spend during the course of the month. This includes allocating funds for essential categories such as housing, utilities, groceries, transportation, entertainment, and any other anticipated expenses.

Step 3: Analyzing Real-World Expenditure: At the end of the month, engage in an exercise of tracking your actual spending across various expense categories. This crucial step allows you to ascertain how closely your financial reality aligns with your initial budgetary projections.

Step 4: Prepare for Astonishing Revelations: As you compare your Total Monthly Income against both your Total Monthly Expenses and your Total Actual Spending, you may find yourself astounded. This insightful exercise often unveils a stark contrast between your perception of spending and the fiscal reality you have experienced.

Step 5: Harness the Power of Budgeting: Budgeting serves as a formidable instrument to commandeer your financial destiny. By consistently monitoring your income and expenses, you empower yourself to make informed financial decisions. As a result, you pave the way for building wealth and achieving the financial prosperity you aspire to attain."

MONTHLY INCOME AND EXPENSES WORKSHEET

Monthly Income Per Month

Products   _____ $_____

Services   _____ $_____

Other Income

Bonus $_____

Commission $_____

Grants $_____

Other $_____ $_____

Other $_____ $_____

Total Income $_____

BUDGETING BUILDS WEALTH

Use the form below to create your monthly budget. Start by writing down what you plan to spend for the month. At the end of the month, write in what you actually spent for the month and then compare the two lists. You will be amazed at how much you think you are spending compared to what you are actually have spent.

Monthly Expenses	Budget	Actual
Salary	_____	_____
Mortgage or Rent	_____	_____
Insurance	_____	_____
Appliance Payments	_____	_____
Cable	_____	_____
Taxes	_____	_____
Electricity	_____	_____
Gas	_____	_____
Water	_____	_____
Trash/Recycle/Sewage	_____	_____
Telephone (Office)	_____	_____
Cell Phone	_____	_____
Internet	_____	_____
Office Maintenance	_____	_____
Food (Eating Out)	_____	_____
Automobile Payment	_____	_____

Gas and Oil   _____   _____

Car Insurance   _____   _____

License   _____   _____

Automobile Repairs   _____   _____

Life Insurance   _____   _____

Medical Insurance   _____   _____

Childcare   _____   _____

Savings/Investments   _____   _____

Clothing   _____   _____

Dry Cleaning/Laundry   _____   _____

Printing   _____   _____

Office/Cleaning Supplies   _____   _____

Tuition/Education   _____   _____

Dues/Memberships   _____   _____

Gifts   _____   _____

Apps/Subscriptions   _____   _____

Books and Magazines   _____   _____

Entertainment   _____   _____

Travel   _____   _____

Marketing and Advertising   _____   _____

Total Expenses $_____ $_____

FINANCIAL REALITY TOTAL

Monthly Income $_____

       Subtract

Total Expenses $_____

      Surplus + $_____

      Deficit - $_____

Do you have a surplus or a deficit at the end of the month?

_____Surplus   _____Deficit

If you are spending more than you earn, there are some major changes that need to take place.

How can you increase your income?

1.   6.

2.   7.

3.   8.

4.   9.

5.   10.

How can you cut your spending? What are the items that you can do without?

1.   6.

2.   7.

3.   8.

4.   9.

5.   10.

TRACK YOUR SPENDING

It's very important that you track your spending on this journey. You must be aware of where each and every penny is going. Use the forms below to track your daily spending. The goal is to get rid of wasteful spending and plan for your financial future.

DAILY SPENDING RECORD
OCTOBER 2025

Week Start Date: _____   **Week End Date:** _____

Date:	Amount:	Date:	Amount:
Item:		Item:	
Date:	Amount:	Date:	Amount:
Item:		Item:	
Date:	Amount:	Date:	Amount:
Item:		Item:	
Date:	Amount:	Date:	Amount:
Item:		Item:	
Date:	Amount:	Date:	Amount:
Item:		Item:	
Date:	Amount:	Date:	Amount:
Item:		Item:	
Number of Items for the Day:		**Total Amount Spent:**	

DAILY SPENDING RECORD
OCTOBER 2025

Week Start Date: _____   **Week End Date:** _____

Date: Amount: Item:	Date: Amount: Item:
Date: Amount: Item:	Date: Amount: Item:
Date: Amount: Item:	Date: Amount: Item:
Date: Amount: Item:	Date: Amount: Item:
Date: Amount: Item:	Date: Amount: Item:
Date: Amount: Item:	Date: Amount: Item:
Number of Items for the Day:	**Total Amount Spent:**

DAILY SPENDING RECORD
OCTOBER 2025

Week Start Date: _____   **Week End Date:** _____

Date: Amount: Item:	Date: Amount: Item:
Date: Amount: Item:	Date: Amount: Item:
Date: Amount: Item:	Date: Amount: Item:
Date: Amount: Item:	Date: Amount: Item:
Date: Amount: Item:	Date: Amount: Item:
Date: Amount: Item:	Date: Amount: Item:
Number of Items for the Day:	**Total Amount Spent:**

DAILY SPENDING RECORD
OCTOBER 2025

Week Start Date: _____   **Week End Date:** _____

Date: Amount:	Date: Amount:
Item:	Item:
Date: Amount: Item:	Date: Amount: Item:
Date: Amount: Item:	Date: Amount: Item:
Date: Amount: Item:	Date: Amount: Item:
Date: Amount: Item:	Date: Amount: Item:
Date: Amount: Item:	Date: Amount: Item:
Number of Items for the Day:	**Total Amount Spent:**

DAILY SPENDING RECORD
OCTOBER 2025

Week Start Date: _____   **Week End Date:** _____

Date: Amount:	Date: Amount:
Item:	Item:
Date: Amount: Item:	Date: Amount: Item:
Date: Amount: Item:	Date: Amount: Item:
Date: Amount: Item:	Date: Amount: Item:
Date: Amount: Item:	Date: Amount: Item:
Date: Amount: Item:	Date: Amount: Item:
Number of Items for the Day:	**Total Amount Spent:**

Set a goal to make 2025 the year of abundance. Use the form below to track every penny that you're receiving. It's amazing that when your mind is focused on abundance, you begin to create abundance.

DAILY INCOME RECORD
OCTOBER 2025

	Date	Source	Amount
1			
2			
3			
4			
5			
6			
7			
8			
9			
10			
11			
12			
13			
14			
15			
16			
17			
18			
19			
20			
21			
22			
23			
24			
25			
26			
27			
28			
29			
30			
31			

CULTIVATE AN ATTITUDE OF GRATITUDE

Everyday take 10 to 15 minutes to write down a few things you are grateful for. Don't just write things down really feel what you are writing. The more grateful you are the more financial blessings will come your way. I am speaking from my own experience. Try it, it really works.

1. _____
2. _____
3. _____
4. _____
5. _____
6. _____
7. _____
8. _____
9. _____
10. _____
11. _____
12. _____
13. _____
14. _____
15. _____
16. _____
17. _____
18. _____
19. _____
20 _____

NOVEMBER 2025

Financial Goal for November 2025: _____

_____

SUN	MON	TUE	WED	THU	FRI	SAT
						1
2	3	4	5	6	7	8
9	10	11	12	13	14	15
16	17	18	19	20	21	22
23	24	25	26	27	28	29
30						

SIX DAILY EMPOWERING QUESTIONS TO BOOST YOUR INCOME

Question 1: Discover Hidden Treasures: Each day, embark on a treasure hunt within your life. Ask yourself: What valuable possessions or assets can I offer for sale today? Share these gems on digital marketplaces and enlist the support of your warm network of friends and family to help you broadcast the news. Their assistance can be the catalyst for spreading the word far and wide.

_____

_____

_____

Question 2: Settle Past Accounts: Revisit your financial history and remind yourself of any outstanding debts owed to you. Reach out to these individuals and ensure that you collect what is rightfully yours.

_____

_____

_____

Question 3: Crafting Value to Share: Explore your artistic side and inquire: What valuable creations can I craft to share with others? Think about crafting handmade goods or offering digital prints as prime examples of how your creativity can translate into financial gains.

_____

_____

_____

_____

Question 4: Unleash Your Skills for Profit: Unleash your inner entrepreneur by pondering the following: What simple services can I provide in exchange for income? Consider your unique abilities, from mowing lawns and providing handyman services to diving into social media marketing, making calls, offering business coaching, consulting services, or administrative wizardry. Capitalize on your talents that have garnered admiration, as they can swiftly translate into a source of cash flow.

_____

_____

_____

Question 5: Solve Problems for Profit: Channel your creativity by asking: What common problems can I effortlessly solve? Identify your exceptional qualifications, talents, and skills that can be harnessed to generate swift income.

_____

_____

_____

Question 6: Trust in Networking: Lastly, consider your network of trustworthy connections. Is there someone you trust, and who trusts you, from whom you can secure a short-term loan if needed? Building on established relationships can provide vital financial support when you need it most.

_____

_____

_____

Your daily engagement with these questions can be a transformative step towards enhancing your financial well-being. Embrace the opportunity to unlock your financial potential!"

UNLOCKING FINANCIAL PROSPERITY THROUGH BUDGETING

Welcome to the path of financial empowerment. To take control of your financial destiny, harness the power of budgeting with the following guidance:

Step 1: Crafting Your Monthly Budget: Begin your journey by utilizing the form provided to create a comprehensive monthly budget. Initiate the process by documenting all your sources of income, leaving no potential revenue stream unaccounted for.

Step 2: Financial Planning: Start by being very clear about what you intend to spend during the course of the month. This includes allocating funds for essential categories such as housing, utilities, groceries, transportation, entertainment, and any other anticipated expenses.

Step 3: Analyzing Real-World Expenditure: At the end of the month, engage in an exercise of tracking your actual spending across various expense categories. This crucial step allows you to ascertain how closely your financial reality aligns with your initial budgetary projections.

Step 4: Prepare for Astonishing Revelations: As you compare your Total Monthly Income against both your Total Monthly Expenses and your Total Actual Spending, you may find yourself astounded. This insightful exercise often unveils a stark contrast between your perception of spending and the fiscal reality you have experienced.

Step 5: Harness the Power of Budgeting: Budgeting serves as a formidable instrument to commandeer your financial destiny. By consistently monitoring your income and expenses, you empower yourself to make informed financial decisions. As a result, you pave the way for building wealth and achieving the financial prosperity you aspire to attain."

MONTHLY INCOME AND EXPENSES WORKSHEET

Monthly Income Per Month

Products   _____ $_____

Services   _____ $_____

Other Income

Bonus $_____

Commission $_____

Grants $_____

Other $_____ $_____

Other $_____ $_____

Total Income $_____

BUDGETING BUILDS WEALTH

Use the form below to create your monthly budget. Start by writing down what you plan to spend for the month. At the end of the month, write in what you actually spent for the month and then compare the two lists. You will be amazed at how much you think you are spending compared to what you are actually have spent.

Monthly Expenses	Budget	Actual
Salary	_____	_____
Mortgage or Rent	_____	_____
Insurance	_____	_____
Appliance Payments	_____	_____
Cable	_____	_____
Taxes	_____	_____
Electricity	_____	_____
Gas	_____	_____
Water	_____	_____
Trash/Recycle/Sewage	_____	_____
Telephone (Office)	_____	_____
Cell Phone	_____	_____
Internet	_____	_____
Office Maintenance	_____	_____
Food (Eating Out)	_____	_____
Automobile Payment	_____	_____

Gas and Oil	_____	_____
Car Insurance	_____	_____
License	_____	_____
Automobile Repairs	_____	_____
Life Insurance	_____	_____
Medical Insurance	_____	_____
Childcare	_____	_____
Savings/Investments	_____	_____
Clothing	_____	_____
Dry Cleaning/Laundry	_____	_____
Printing	_____	_____
Office/Cleaning Supplies	_____	_____
Tuition/Education	_____	_____
Dues/Memberships	_____	_____
Gifts	_____	_____
Apps/Subscriptions	_____	_____
Books and Magazines	_____	_____
Entertainment	_____	_____
Travel	_____	_____
Marketing and Advertising	_____	_____
Total Expenses	$_____	$_____

FINANCIAL REALITY TOTAL

Monthly Income $_____

Subtract

Total Expenses $_____

Surplus + $_____

Deficit - $_____

Do you have a surplus or a deficit at the end of the month?

_____Surplus   _____Deficit

If you are spending more than you earn, there are some major changes that need to take place.

How can you increase your income?

1.   6.

2.   7.

3.   8.

4.   9.

5.   10.

How can you cut your spending? What are the items that you can do without?

1.   6.

2.   7.

3.   8.

4.   9.

5.   10.

TRACK YOUR SPENDING

It's very important that you track your spending on this journey. You must be aware of where each and every penny is going. Use the forms below to track your daily spending. The goal is to get rid of wasteful spending and plan for your financial future.

DAILY SPENDING RECORD
NOVEMBER 2025

Week Start Date: _____ **Week End Date:** _____

Date:	Amount:	Date:	Amount:
Item:		Item:	
Date:	Amount:	Date:	Amount:
Item:		Item:	
Date:	Amount:	Date:	Amount:
Item:		Item:	
Date:	Amount:	Date:	Amount:
Item:		Item:	
Date:	Amount:	Date:	Amount:
Item:		Item:	
Date:	Amount:	Date:	Amount:
Item:		Item:	
Number of Items for the Day:		**Total Amount Spent:**	

DAILY SPENDING RECORD
NOVEMBER 2025

Week Start Date: _____ **Week End Date:** _____

Date: Amount: Item:	Date: Amount: Item:
Date: Amount: Item:	Date: Amount: Item:
Date: Amount: Item:	Date: Amount: Item:
Date: Amount: Item:	Date: Amount: Item:
Date: Amount: Item:	Date: Amount: Item:
Date: Amount: Item:	Date: Amount: Item:
Number of Items for the Day:	**Total Amount Spent:**

DAILY SPENDING RECORD
NOVEMBER 2025

Week Start Date: _____ **Week End Date:** _____

Date: Amount: Item:	Date: Amount: Item:
Date: Amount: Item:	Date: Amount: Item:
Date: Amount: Item:	Date: Amount: Item:
Date: Amount: Item:	Date: Amount: Item:
Date: Amount: Item:	Date: Amount: Item:
Date: Amount: Item:	Date: Amount: Item:
Number of Items for the Day:	**Total Amount Spent:**

DAILY SPENDING RECORD
NOVEMBER 2025

Week Start Date: _____ **Week End Date:** _____

Date: Item:	Amount:	Date: Item:	Amount:
Date: Item:	Amount:	Date: Item:	Amount:
Date: Item:	Amount:	Date: Item:	Amount:
Date: Item:	Amount:	Date: Item:	Amount:
Date: Item:	Amount:	Date: Item:	Amount:
Date: Item:	Amount:	Date: Item:	Amount:
Number of Items for the Day:		**Total Amount Spent:**	

DAILY SPENDING RECORD
NOVEMBER 2025

Week Start Date: _____ **Week End Date:** _____

Date: Item:	Amount:	Date: Item:	Amount:
Date: Item:	Amount:	Date: Item:	Amount:
Date: Item:	Amount:	Date: Item:	Amount:
Date: Item:	Amount:	Date: Item:	Amount:
Date: Item:	Amount:	Date: Item:	Amount:
Date: Item:	Amount:	Date: Item:	Amount:
Number of Items for the Day:		**Total Amount Spent:**	

Set a goal to make 2025 the year of abundance. Use the form below to track every penny that you're receiving. It's amazing that when your mind is focused on abundance, you begin to create abundance.

DAILY INCOME RECORD
NOVEMBER 2025

	Date	Source	Amount
1			
2			
3			
4			
5			
6			
7			
8			
9			
10			
11			
12			
13			
14			
15			
16			
17			
18			
19			
20			
21			
22			
23			
24			
25			
26			
27			
28			
29			
30			

CULTIVATE AN ATTITUDE OF GRATITUDE

Everyday take 10 to 15 minutes to write down a few things you are grateful for. Don't just write things down really feel what you are writing. The more grateful you are the more financial blessings will come your way. I am speaking from my own experience. Try it, it really works.

1. _____
2. _____
3. _____
4. _____
5. _____
6. _____
7. _____
8. _____
9. _____
10. _____
11. _____
12. _____
13. _____
14. _____
15. _____
16. _____
17. _____
18. _____
19. _____
20 _____

DECEMBER 2025

Financial Goal for December 2025: _____

_____

SUN	MON	TUE	WED	THU	FRI	SAT
		1	2	3	4	5	6
7	8	9	10	11	12	13
14	15	16	17	18	19	20
21	22	23	24	25	26	27
28	29	30	31			

SIX DAILY EMPOWERING QUESTIONS TO BOOST YOUR INCOME

Question 1: Discover Hidden Treasures: Each day, embark on a treasure hunt within your life. Ask yourself: What valuable possessions or assets can I offer for sale today? Share these gems on digital marketplaces and enlist the support of your warm network of friends and family to help you broadcast the news. Their assistance can be the catalyst for spreading the word far and wide.

_____

_____

_____

Question 2: Settle Past Accounts: Revisit your financial history and remind yourself of any outstanding debts owed to you. Reach out to these individuals and ensure that you collect what is rightfully yours.

_____

_____

_____

Question 3: Crafting Value to Share: Explore your artistic side and inquire: What valuable creations can I craft to share with others? Think about crafting handmade goods or offering digital prints as prime examples of how your creativity can translate into financial gains.

_____

_____

_____

_____

Question 4: Unleash Your Skills for Profit: Unleash your inner entrepreneur by pondering the following: What simple services can I provide in exchange for income? Consider your unique abilities, from mowing lawns and providing handyman services to diving into social media marketing, making calls, offering business coaching, consulting services, or administrative wizardry. Capitalize on your talents that have garnered admiration, as they can swiftly translate into a source of cash flow.

_____

_____

_____

Question 5: Solve Problems for Profit: Channel your creativity by asking: What common problems can I effortlessly solve? Identify your exceptional qualifications, talents, and skills that can be harnessed to generate swift income.

_____

_____

_____

Question 6: Trust in Networking: Lastly, consider your network of trustworthy connections. Is there someone you trust, and who trusts you, from whom you can secure a short-term loan if needed? Building on established relationships can provide vital financial support when you need it most.

_____

_____

_____

Your daily engagement with these questions can be a transformative step towards enhancing your financial well-being. Embrace the opportunity to unlock your financial potential!"

UNLOCKING FINANCIAL PROSPERITY THROUGH BUDGETING

Welcome to the path of financial empowerment. To take control of your financial destiny, harness the power of budgeting with the following guidance:

Step 1: Crafting Your Monthly Budget: Begin your journey by utilizing the form provided to create a comprehensive monthly budget. Initiate the process by documenting all your sources of income, leaving no potential revenue stream unaccounted for.

Step 2: Financial Planning: Start by being very clear about what you intend to spend during the course of the month. This includes allocating funds for essential categories such as housing, utilities, groceries, transportation, entertainment, and any other anticipated expenses.

Step 3: Analyzing Real-World Expenditure: At the end of the month, engage in an exercise of tracking your actual spending across various expense categories. This crucial step allows you to ascertain how closely your financial reality aligns with your initial budgetary projections.

Step 4: Prepare for Astonishing Revelations: As you compare your Total Monthly Income against both your Total Monthly Expenses and your Total Actual Spending, you may find yourself astounded. This insightful exercise often unveils a stark contrast between your perception of spending and the fiscal reality you have experienced.

Step 5: Harness the Power of Budgeting: Budgeting serves as a formidable instrument to commandeer your financial destiny. By consistently monitoring your income and expenses, you empower yourself to make informed financial decisions. As a result, you pave the way for building wealth and achieving the financial prosperity you aspire to attain."

MONTHLY INCOME AND EXPENSES WORKSHEET

Monthly Income Per Month

Products   _____ $_____

Services   _____ $_____

Other Income

Bonus $_____

Commission $_____

Grants $_____

Other $_____ $_____

Other $_____ $_____

Total Income $_____

BUDGETING BUILDS WEALTH

Use the form below to create your monthly budget. Start by writing down what you plan to spend for the month. At the end of the month, write in what you actually spent for the month and then compare the two lists. You will be amazed at how much you think you are spending compared to what you are actually have spent.

Monthly Expenses	Budget	Actual
Salary	_____	_____
Mortgage or Rent	_____	_____
Insurance	_____	_____
Appliance Payments	_____	_____
Cable	_____	_____
Taxes	_____	_____
Electricity	_____	_____
Gas	_____	_____
Water	_____	_____
Trash/Recycle/Sewage	_____	_____
Telephone (Office)	_____	_____
Cell Phone	_____	_____
Internet	_____	_____
Office Maintenance	_____	_____
Food (Eating Out)	_____	_____
Automobile Payment	_____	_____

Gas and Oil	_____	_____
Car Insurance	_____	_____
License	_____	_____
Automobile Repairs	_____	_____
Life Insurance	_____	_____
Medical Insurance	_____	_____
Childcare	_____	_____
Savings/Investments	_____	_____
Clothing	_____	_____
Dry Cleaning/Laundry	_____	_____
Printing	_____	_____
Office/Cleaning Supplies	_____	_____
Tuition/Education	_____	_____
Dues/Memberships	_____	_____
Gifts	_____	_____
Apps/Subscriptions	_____	_____
Books and Magazines	_____	_____
Entertainment	_____	_____
Travel	_____	_____
Marketing and Advertising	_____	_____
Total Expenses	$_____	$_____

FINANCIAL REALITY TOTAL

Monthly Income $_____

         Subtract

Total Expenses $_____

       Surplus + $_____

       Deficit - $_____

Do you have a surplus or a deficit at the end of the month?

_____Surplus   _____Deficit

If you are spending more than you earn, there are some major changes that need to take place.

How can you increase your income?

1.   6.

2.   7.

3.   8.

4.   9.

5.   10.

How can you cut your spending? What are the items that you can do without?

1.   6.

2.   7.

3.   8.

4.   9.

5.   10.

TRACK YOUR SPENDING

It's very important that you track your spending on this journey. You must be aware of where each and every penny is going. Use the forms below to track your daily spending. The goal is to get rid of wasteful spending and plan for your financial future.

DAILY SPENDING RECORD
DECEMBER 2025

Week Start Date: _____   **Week End Date:** _____

Date: Amount: Item:		Date: Amount: Item:
Date: Amount: Item:		Date: Amount: Item:
Date: Amount: Item:		Date: Amount: Item:
Date: Amount: Item:		Date: Amount: Item:
Date: Amount: Item:		Date: Amount: Item:
Date: Amount: Item:		Date: Amount: Item:
Number of Items for the Day:		**Total Amount Spent:**

DAILY SPENDING RECORD
DECEMBER 2025

Week Start Date: _____   **Week End Date:** _____

Date:	Amount:	Date:	Amount:
Item:		Item:	
Date:	Amount:	Date:	Amount:
Item:		Item:	
Date:	Amount:	Date:	Amount:
Item:		Item:	
Date:	Amount:	Date:	Amount:
Item:		Item:	
Date:	Amount:	Date:	Amount:
Item:		Item:	
Date:	Amount:	Date:	Amount:
Item:		Item:	
Number of Items for the Day:		**Total Amount Spent:**	

DAILY SPENDING RECORD
DECEMBER 2025

Week Start Date: _____   **Week End Date:** _____

Date:	Amount:	Date:	Amount:
Item:		Item:	
Date:	Amount:	Date:	Amount:
Item:		Item:	
Date:	Amount:	Date:	Amount:
Item:		Item:	
Date:	Amount:	Date:	Amount:
Item:		Item:	
Date:	Amount:	Date:	Amount:
Item:		Item:	
Date:	Amount:	Date:	Amount:
Item:		Item:	
Number of Items for the Day:		**Total Amount Spent:**	

DAILY SPENDING RECORD
DECEMBER 2025

Week Start Date: _____   **Week End Date:** _____

Date: Item:	Amount:	Date: Item:	Amount:
Date: Item:	Amount:	Date: Item:	Amount:
Date: Item:	Amount:	Date: Item:	Amount:
Date: Item:	Amount:	Date: Item:	Amount:
Date: Item:	Amount:	Date: Item:	Amount:
Date: Item:	Amount:	Date: Item:	Amount:
Number of Items for the Day:		**Total Amount Spent:**	

DAILY SPENDING RECORD
DECEMBER 2025

Week Start Date: _____   **Week End Date:** _____

Date: Item:	Amount:	Date: Item:	Amount:
Date: Item:	Amount:	Date: Item:	Amount:
Date: Item:	Amount:	Date: Item:	Amount:
Date: Item:	Amount:	Date: Item:	Amount:
Date: Item:	Amount:	Date: Item:	Amount:
Date: Item:	Amount:	Date: Item:	Amount:
Number of Items for the Day:		**Total Amount Spent:**	

Set a goal to make 2025 the year of abundance. Use the form below to track every penny that you're receiving. It's amazing that when your mind is focused on abundance, you begin to create abundance.

DAILY INCOME RECORD
DECEMBER 2025

	Date	Source	Amount
1			
2			
3			
4			
5			
6			
7			
8			
9			
10			
11			
12			
13			
14			
15			
16			
17			
18			
19			
20			
21			
22			
23			
24			
25			
26			
27			
28			
29			
30			
31			

CULTIVATE AN ATTITUDE OF GRATITUDE

Everyday take 10 to 15 minutes to write down a few things you are grateful for. Don't just write things down really feel what you are writing. The more grateful you are the more financial blessings will come your way. I am speaking from my own experience. Try it, it really works.

1. _____
2. _____
3. _____
4. _____
5. _____
6. _____
7. _____
8. _____
9. _____
10. _____
11. _____
12. _____
13. _____
14. _____
15. _____
16. _____
17. _____
18. _____
19. _____
20 _____

2025 Calendar and Financial Empowerment Tool

- 2025 Calendar
- Monthly Financial Empowerment Affirmations
- 20 Ways to Increase Your Income
- Six Daily Empowering Questions to Boost Your Income
- Monthly Budget forms
- Daily Spending Tracking forms
- Daily Income Tracking forms

To order the 2025 Financial Empowerment Calendar in bulk contact:

Business Coach Renee Bobb
(615) 753-5647
reneebobbtraining@gmail.com
www.ReneeBobbTraining.com
www.stan.store/reneebobbtraining
www.GrantFundingAcademy.com

Business Coach Renee is available to teach Financial Empowerment Workshops, Webinars, and Seminars. She also offers one-on-one customized Financial Empowerment Coaching Services.

Use this QR Code to Learn more about
Renee Bobb Training LLC.

Receive additional services, get access to additional
resources, and purchase other books.

SCAN ME

Made in the USA
Middletown, DE
16 April 2025

74324334R00099